IT COULD BE ANY ONE OF US

A Comedy

by Alan Ayckbourn

SAMUEL FRENCH

samuelfrench.co.uk

ISBN 978-0-573-01797-1

www.samuelfrench.co.uk
www.samuelfrench.com

FOR AMATEUR PRODUCTION ENQUIRIES

UNITED KINGDOM AND WORLD
EXCLUDING NORTH AMERICA
plays@samuelfrench.co.uk
020 7255 4302/01

Each title is subject to availability from Samuel French, depending upon country of performance.

Other plays by ALAN AYCKBOURN
published and licensed by Samuel French

Absent Friends

Arrivals and Departures

Awaking Beauty

Bedroom Farce

Body Language

Callisto 5

The Champion of Paribanou

A Chorus of Disapproval

Comic Potential

Communicating Doors

Confusions

A Cut in the Rates

Dreams from a Summer House

Drowning on Dry Land

Ernie's Incredible Illucinations

Family Circles

Farcicals

FlatSpin

GamePlan

Gizmo

Haunting Julia

Henceforward

Hero’s Welcome

House & Garden

How the Other Half Loves

If I Were You

Improbable Fiction

Intimate Exchanges, Volume I

Intimate Exchanges, Volume II

Joking Apart

Just Between Ourselves

Life and Beth

Life of Riley

Living Together

Me, Myself and I

Man of the Moment

Mixed Doubles

Mr. A’s Amazing Maze Plays

Mr Whatnot

My Very Own Story

My Wonderful Day

Neighbourhood Watch

The Norman Conquests: Table Manners; Living Together; Round and Round the Garden

Private Fears in Public Places

Relatively Speaking

The Revengers' Comedies

RolePlay

Roundelay

Season's Greetings

Sisterly Feelings

A Small Family Business

Snake in the Grass

Suburban Strains

Sugar Daddies

Taking Steps

Ten Times Table

Things We Do for Love

This Is Where We Came In

Time and Time Again

Time of My Life

Tons of Money (revised)

Way Upstream

Wildest Dreams

Wolf at the Door

Woman in Mind

A Word from Our Sponsor

Other plays by ALAN AYCKBOURN licensed by Samuel French

The Boy Who Fell Into a Book

Invisible Friends

The Jollies

Orvin – Champion of Champions

Surprises

Whenever

ABOUT THE AUTHOR

Alan Ayckbourn has worked in theatre as a playwright and director for over fifty years, rarely if ever tempted by television or film, which perhaps explains why he continues to be so prolific. To date he has written more than seventy-nine plays, many one act plays and a large amount of work for the younger audience. His work has been translated into over thirty-five languages, is performed on stage and television throughout the world and has won countless awards.

Major successes include: *Relatively Speaking, How the Other Half Loves, Absurd Person Singular, Bedroom Farce, A Chorus of Disapproval,* and *The Norman Conquests.* In recent years, there have been revivals of *Season's Greetings* and *A Small Family Business* at the National theatre, in the West End *Absent Friends, A Chorus of Disapproval, Relatively Speaking* and *How the Other Half Loves.* In 2015, Chichester mounted a very successful revival of *Way Upstream.*

Artistic Director of the Stephen Joseph theatre from 1972 to 2009 where almost all his plays have been first staged, he continues to direct his latest new work there. In recent years, he has been inducted into American Theatre's Hall of Fame, received the 2010 Critics' Circle Award for Services to the Arts and became the first British playwright to receive both Olivier and Tony Special Lifetime Achievement Awards. He was knighted in 1997 for services to the theatre.

Image credit: Andrew Higgins.

AUTHOR'S NOTE

After a lifetime of playwriting (I first started as an unpublished writer at the age of ten!) my career has moved steadily forward from the status of untried tyro through to establishment figure to ageing experimentalist!

The work has reflected this. From the early tried and tested plays, (*Relatively Speaking, How the Other Half Loves, The Norman Conquests*, etc.) which thankfully people still seem happy to produce and come to see, through the middle period, larger scale so called "social" pieces (*Man of the Moment, A Chorus of Disapproval*) to the more recent smaller scale departures such as *Private Fears in Public Places, Snake in the Grass* and *Haunting Julia*, I have continued to experiment with shape and form, whilst I hope continuing to deepen my characters.

Throughout this, though, I have always needed to remind myself of the overriding prime directive drummed into me at an early age by my mentor, Stephen Joseph, that above all else a playwright is a storyteller.

To keep an audience in their seats you need to involve them in a constantly unfolding series of unexpected twists and turns. These can, of course, be the narrative of the story itself as in *Relatively Speaking* or, as with *Woman in Mind* say, through the psychological development of the characters.

One of the nicest things people can ever say to me, coming out of a new play for the first time of seeing it, is "Well, I never saw THAT coming!"

Alan Ayckbourn

IT COULD BE ANY ONE OF US

First performed at the Stephen Joseph Theatre in the Round, Scarborough, on 5th October 1983, with the following cast:

MORTIMER CHALKE	Graeme Eton
JOCELYN POLEGATE	Ursula Jones
BRINTON CHALKE	Robin Herford
AMY POLEGATE	Liza Sadovy
NORRIS HONEYWELL	John Arthur
WENDY WINDWOOD	Lavinia Bertram

Directed by Alan Ayckbourn
Designed by Edward Lipscomb
Lighting by Francis Lynch
Music by Paul Todd

Subsequently performed in this revised version at the Stephen Joseph Theatre on 20th August 1996, with the following cast:

MORTIMER CHALKE	Malcolm Rennie
JOCELYN POLEGATE	Juliet Mills
BRINTON CHALKE	Richard Derrington
AMY POLEGATE	Tabitha Wady
NORRIS HONEYWELL	Jon Strickland
WENDY WINDWOOD	Janet Dibley

Directed by Alan Ayckbourn
Designed by Roger Glossop
Lighting by Mick Hughes
Music by John Pattison

CHARACTERS

MORTIMER CHALKE: a composer; mid-fifties
JOCELYN POLEGATE: a writer, his sister; late forties
BRINTON CHALKE: a painter, his brother; early forties
AMY POLEGATE: Jocelyn's daughter; sixteen
NORRIS HONEYWELL: a detective, mid-forties
WENDY WINDWOOD: mid-thirties

The action of the play takes place in the hall/sitting-room of the Chalke family residence during a fortnight in January

ACT I

Scene One	Monday evening at about 5.30 p.m.
Scene Two	Saturday evening at about 5.30 p.m., two weeks later

ACT II

Scene One	That same Saturday night at about 9 p.m.
Scene Two	The next day, Sunday morning, at about 11.30 a.m.

NOTES

The Ending

There are three alternative endings built into the play.

It is possible that, depending on small textual alterations, either **Jocelyn** or **Amy** or **Brinton** could have committed the crime. This can either be pre-decided and arranged or, more interestingly, the card game at the end of ACT I Scene One can be used to pre-select the guilty party at random – depending on who gets a certain card.

In any event, if it should be **Brinton**, then the section on page 63 between +++ and +++ should be excluded and the section on page 100 between +++ and +++ should be included and the first alternative ending played.

If it should be **Amy**, then the section on page 94 between ••• and ••• and the section on pages 97 between ••• and ••• should be included and the second alternative ending played.

If it should be **Jocelyn**, then the section on pages 89 – 90 between *** and *** and the section on page 92 between *** and *** should be included and the third alternative ending played.

Interrupted Speeches

A speech usually follows the one before it BUT:

When one character starts speaking before the other has finished, the point of interruption is marked /.

e.g. **NORRIS** You want me to stand outside in the pouring rain while he plays the piano, fine. / Next time, I will do. I'm so sorry.

JOCELYN All I'm saying is when you saw he was playing the piano, / the least you could have done was to show a little—

NORRIS I'm so, so sorry.

ACT I

Scene One

The hall/sitting-room of the CHALKES' *family residence somewhere in rural Northern England. Monday evening. About 5.30 p.m.*

The house itself is a large stone built Victorian folly, built at a time when money was plentiful and when servants and fuel bills were cheap. Some hundred years later it has become very run down and in need of refurbishment. There are, however, still a few indications of how it must have looked even twenty years ago when old man CHALKE *was alive. The furnishings are substantial if shabby. A fine ornate fireplace, still practical but at present adorned with a totally inadequate electric fire. A table to seat at least six though probably extendable to seat sixteen. In one corner, a good quality grand piano, again having seen better days, with a piano stool. A sideboard. One or two comfortable armchairs and possibly a sofa. Impressive, if rather draughty, high windows, expensively but shabbily curtained, that look out over the remains of a once-splendid lawn and trees, and part of a gravel drive. The exits from this high room include a solid front door leading directly to the outside; another door across the room leading to the rest of the formal downstairs area including an unseen study, dining-room and billiard room; another, less evident door, possibly even a concealed one, leading to the kitchen and servants' area; finally, a rather impressive flight of stairs leading directly up via a landing to all the upstairs rooms. Overall, we have a feeling of size and a now-faded attempt to recapture a forgotten or perhaps a partially ill-remembered grandeur. Today, anyway, on ground floor level, the family, for practical reasons, have adapted this room into a general-purpose living area.*

The curtain rises on darkness. Before we see anything, we first hear the piano being played; a piece unfamiliar to us, in style perhaps best charitably described as of the modern school. It is quite dramatic with sudden flurried runs of notes, followed by a series of thick, dark chords punctuated rather too often perhaps by lengthy silences. The lights come up. It is a dark, cold, wet evening. We are now able to see the player of the piece – no less than the composer himself, MORTIMER CHALKE, *a red-faced, rather fiery man in his middle fifties. He is playing with great concentration and feeling, eyes closed, with only the most occasional glance at the rough hand-written score in front of him. Listening to this are an audience of three. First, his younger sister,* JOCELYN POLGATE *née* CHALKE, *now in her late forties. She is a rather wispy, hand-knitted sort of woman but, like all the* CHALKES, *displays an unexpected strength of personality, particularly when you least expect it. She is listening at present with all the attention she can muster. Giving the proceedings slightly less of his attention is their younger brother,* BRINTON CHALKE, *a pale, lean, nervous and rather restless man in his early forties. In manner, he is inclined to veer between fits of childlike passion and middle-aged gloom. His eyes are at present darting round the room and it is doubtful, in truth, if he is even hearing the music. The third member of the trio is* AMY *(Amaryllis)* POLEGATE, JOCELYN*'s daughter, aged about sixteen.* AMY *sits to one side of the room wearing her normal expression, a mixture of bored, blank, lowering resentment, the sort of resentment that only a teenager with problems could harbour. She is dumpy and overweight and whilst not altogether unattractive,* *gives the unfortunate impression of having made only half an effort.* **MORTIMER** *continues his recital, giving us a chance to study them all. He reaches another passage in the music punctuated by silences.*

During one of these silences we hear the swift rattle of a Yale key being inserted in the front door. Almost immediately, this swings violently and unexpectedly open. A sharp gust of wind, a flurry of rain and into the doorway blows **NORRIS HONEYWELL**, *a sad-eyed mournful man in his forties. He clutches a soaking umbrella but, despite this, his mac and shoes are sodden.*

The wind catches **MORTIMER**'*s sheets of music and they flutter on the piano. He steadies the score but doesn't otherwise react, refusing to allow his concentration to be broken.*

NORRIS *(blowing the rain off his face, loudly)* Whor! It's fair pissing down out there, you know.

He closes the door.

JOCELYN
BRINTON } *(together)* Ssh!

AMY *stares at him.*

NORRIS *(looking puzzled)* Eh?

MORTIMER *rather pointedly plays another chord.*

(realizing what's going on, mouthing apologetically) Ah! Right. Sorry. Yes. Didn't realize. Right.

MORTIMER *continues to play.* **NORRIS** *carefully leans his umbrella in the doorway, leaving it to form a puddle on the floor.* **BRINTON** *watches the puddle grow during the following. With great care,* **NORRIS** *squelches his way across the room towards the kitchen, unbuttoning his coat as he goes.*

NORRIS *leaves the room, but in a moment, returns again, now holding his coat.*

NORRIS *attempts to convey by gestures to* **JOCELYN** *that he requires a coat hanger for his coat.* **JOCELYN** *looks puzzled, failing to interpret his mime, and she is forced, rather irritably, after a second, to rise and go to him in the kitchen doorway. He whispers something to her. She takes the coat from him.*

JOCELYN *goes out to the kitchen.*

NORRIS *squelches back again to the seat* **JOCELYN** *has recently vacated by the fire. He sits and starts to take off his shoes. He indicates to* **AMY** *that he'd like his slippers.*

AMY *gets up without enthusiasm and exits towards the study.*

MORTIMER *plays on.* **NORRIS**, *having removed his socks, hangs them on the fender to dry.* **NORRIS** *feels under the cushion of his chair and pulls out an old newspaper. Having checked the date, he starts to tear it cautiously but nonetheless noisily and then stuff pieces of it into his wet shoes.* **MORTIMER***'s expression grows grimmer.* **NORRIS**, *having stuffed his shoes, rises and props them carefully in front of the electric fire, balancing them delicately against the fender. Meanwhile,* **BRINTON**, *having come to a decision regarding the umbrella, now rises and, taking it in one hand, opens the front door with the other and steps outside, presumably with the intention of shaking off the excess moisture. The wind catches* **MORTIMER***'s music and he stabs at it again. There is a sudden gust of wind and the front door slams shut like a pistol shot.*

BRINTON *is left outside.*

NORRIS, *still at the fire, jumps involuntarily and knocks over the fire-irons.* **MORTIMER**, *in fury, slams shut the lid of the piano. He turns to face the room for the first time. He is somewhat surprised to see only* **NORRIS** *there. He looks at him with intense hatred.*

NORRIS Is that the end, is it?

MORTIMER *(white with rage; in a low voice)* Yes. Yes, it is. That's the last time you'll ever do that to me, Norris. The last time in your life.

NORRIS *(genuinely puzzled)* Sorry?

MORTIMER You're a growth, Norris. You're not a man at all. You're a malignant growth.

NORRIS What are you on about?

JOCELYN *and* **AMY** *reappear in their respective doorways.* **AMY** *carries* **NORRIS***'s bedroom slippers.*

(turning to **JOCELYN** *and* **AMY***)* What's he on about?

MORTIMER I'm going to have you cut out, Norris. I'm going to have you cauterized.

NORRIS Look, I have wet feet. I am drying my shoes. What else am I supposed to do, you stupid pillock?

JOCELYN Norris!

MORTIMER *(advancing menacingly on* **NORRIS***)* What did you call me?

JOCELYN *(with sudden authority)* Mortimer! Norris! Now stop it, both of you, at once.

There is a silence. The two men face each other, glaring. They so nearly came to blows. The tension is broken by a rather apologetic knocking on the front door. **JOCELYN** *looks at* **AMY***, puzzled.* **AMY** *crosses to the front door and opens it.*

BRINTON *enters rather apologetically, still holding the umbrella.*

BRINTON Sorry. I got – locked out. I was listening to see if you'd finished, I... *(He stops, appreciating the situation, and coughs nervously)* I...

MORTIMER I want this so-called detective out of my house. Do you hear me, Jocelyn? I want him out now. Instantly.

JOCELYN He can't go now, Mortimer, don't be silly. It's pouring with rain.

MORTIMER *(smiling and nodding knowingly)* He's got you all on his side, hasn't he? All ganged up against me, aren't you? Safety in numbers. All stand together, there's a chance you can prop each other up. What is it? Jealousy? Has to be, doesn't it? Pathetic bunch of second-rate failures and all you can usefully do is try and destroy the only one with any talent among you. Well, it won't— *(He snatches his music from the piano, tearing it first in half, then quarters, then eighths as he speaks)* – work, you – won't – bring me down, you – Visigoths.

He scatters the paper on the floor and stamps off towards his study.

I'll have you first. I'll bring you down first, every one of you.

MORTIMER *exits.*

JOCELYN *(without any real hope of calling him back)* Mortimer.

NORRIS Well, what about that for behaviour, eh? What about that? Ever seen behaviour like that before? Deranged.

JOCELYN He was playing us his new composition, Norris. You know what he's like when he's doing that. It's not much to ask. The least you could have done was—

NORRIS *(angrily)* All right, all right. You want me to stand outside in the pouring rain while he plays the piano, fine. / Next time, I will do. I'm so sorry.

JOCELYN All I'm saying is when you saw he was playing the piano, / the least you could have done was to show a little—

AMY Here we go again. *(She throws the slippers down by the fire and starts to go out towards the kitchen)*

NORRIS I'm so, so sorry. I didn't know he was playing the piano. I thought he was tuning it.

BRINTON Please, don't start shouting. Please. *(He coughs)*

JOCELYN All right, all right. *(She controls herself)* Put the kettle on for tea, will you, Amy?

AMY *exits, her voice almost, but not quite, out of earshot as she goes.*

AMY Every single bloody evening it's the same.

JOCELYN *(calling after her)* And that's enough of that, please.

BRINTON I wish Mother was alive. *(He coughs)*

JOCELYN Oh, don't you start.

BRINTON She wouldn't have stood for this. She wouldn't have allowed all this argument. And she'd have had him out to start with. *(He indicates* **NORRIS***)*

NORRIS *groans and sits.*

JOCELYN Brinton.

BRINTON Non-productive, that's what she'd have called him.

JOCELYN Brinton, shut up.

BRINTON It's always me that has to shut up, isn't it? Never anyone— *(He breaks off and coughs again)*

JOCELYN Oh, Brin.

BRINTON *(opening the front door)* It always has to be my fault these days, doesn't it? No matter what it is, it's my fault.

BRINTON *exits, coughing furiously. The front door slams behind him.*

Silence.

NORRIS It's good to be home.

JOCELYN I want to speak to you.

NORRIS Oh, don't please, Joss. I've had a hell of a day. Hell of a day.

JOCELYN *(looking towards the front door)* He's not got a coat on. He'll get soaked to the skin. Be in bed again for weeks.

NORRIS He's all right. He'll be in his – what do you call it – his studio.

JOCELYN I think that's even wetter.

A slight pause. **NORRIS** *warms his feet.*

You're going to have to apologize to Mortimer, you know.

NORRIS Why?

JOCELYN Because it's not fair on the rest of us otherwise.

NORRIS I'll apologize when I'm in the wrong.

JOCELYN You were in the wrong.

NORRIS *(getting angry again)* I was not in the wrong.

JOCELYN *(calming him)* All right. Well, you must make allowances then. He's—

NORRIS *(bitterly)* Artistic.

JOCELYN Well, yes – I wasn't going to say that but—

NORRIS Whereas I am an artisan. An untouchable. A pariah. An unclean. I'm the token tone deaf, dyslexic, colour-blind, non-creative member of this community.

JOCELYN No, you're not. *(Gently)* Please, Norrie. Apologize. For me.

NORRIS Again?

JOCELYN Please.

A pause.

NORRIS He is mad, though. Let's get that quite clear. I will apologize but I would like you to recognize that in any normal, sane house your brother would be chained up in the attic.

JOCELYN Very possibly.

NORRIS *(growing depressed suddenly)* Still, who am I to talk, eh? Who am I?

JOCELYN Another bad day?

NORRIS Not really. Just like yesterday. And the same as tomorrow.

JOCELYN Why don't you give it up, Norrie? It's killing you slowly.

NORRIS And do what? What else can I do? Ten years ago, I was the hottest claims assessor that the Pendon Mutual Fire and General ever had. Slightly dodgy claim? Send for Honeywell. Honeywell's your man. You mean the fire was started deliberately? My God, how does he do it? The man's a genius. They used to stand up when I came into the office. Some of them.

JOCELYN Yes.

NORRIS Why did I ever think I could go it alone?

JOCELYN Because I persuaded you you could.

NORRIS No, no, no. It was my decision.

JOCELYN I wanted you to...I wanted— *(She stops)* Oh, don't let's talk about it again.

NORRIS You were writing your books, your detective books, and that took you away from me and I was jealous. That's all it was. I wanted to be the detective in your life. Michael Stonehill.

JOCELYN Martin Stonegate.

NORRIS Right. I wanted to be Martin Stonegate. That's a laugh, isn't it?

JOCELYN Well, you make a good pair, anyway. Martin Stonegate's never solved a case either.

NORRIS He has, he has.

JOCELYN Not really. Thirty-four of them he's started on, poor man. Thirty-four books and I haven't managed to finish writing one of them. I doubt if I ever will now.

NORRIS *(encouragingly)* You will. You've got your – what is it – writer's block, that's all.

JOCELYN *(bitterly)* Martin Stonegate. Master of the unsolved crime.

NORRIS Do you know, I think I could give it up, Joss, if I could only solve just one case. I really could. Just one. Examining the scene of the crime, inspecting the body, narrowing down the suspects, checking the alibis and then, all together in one room, "Ladies and gentlemen, I am about to present to you a murderer." ... "A burglar." ... "The man who nicked my felt tip pen." Anybody.

The phone tings (someone is using an extension elsewhere)

JOCELYN Who could Mortimer be phoning?

NORRIS A psychiatrist?

JOCELYN He very rarely phones. He hates it.

NORRIS At least he's allowed to use it.

JOCELYN It's his house, his phone.

NORRIS And we are not allowed to forget it. Incoming calls only. Terrific. If you're feeling suicidal, you're meant to sit here praying the Samaritans get a wrong number.

JOCELYN Nothing we can do, Norris. It's the same for all of us.

NORRIS It's your house as well. It's yours and Brinton's as well.

JOCELYN Not legally. Father hated women and he thought Brinton was subnormal.

NORRIS Well, I think the day is coming when somebody's going to have to sort him out. *(During the following he picks up the remains of the old newspaper and begins to read)*

JOCELYN Splendid. Then we'll all be out in the street, won't we?

AMY *enters from the kitchen with a tray of tea things which she places and unloads on the table.*

I suppose I'll have to fetch Brinton in a minute. My whole life these days is spent fetching people from various rooms. Bringing them back together again. No wonder I can't write. I never get a minute to myself. I'll give you a hand in a second, Amy.

AMY *(heading for the kitchen; as she goes)* Hooray, hooray, hooray.

AMY *exits with the tray.*

JOCELYN *(ineffectually, calling after* **AMY***)* Don't talk to me like that, Amy. Don't talk to your mother like that.

Silence.

We're going to have to do something about her. We really are.

NORRIS Oh, yes.

JOCELYN We are, Norrie.

NORRIS Don't look at me.

JOCELYN We're both responsible—

NORRIS It's too late now, Joss. You can't ask me to start being a father now. Ten years ago, yes, with pleasure. But no, you didn't want that. Amy didn't want that. Fair enough. Stranger in the home. Understood. But you can't expect me to start now. She's a grown girl. Mind of her own.

JOCELYN *(muttering)* Another thing left to me, is it?

NORRIS *(angrily)* Look, you want a father for her, go and find him. He'll still be there. In his symphony orchestra. Shacked up with half the cello section, no doubt. Go and drag him out of the Birmingham Town Hall. She's his responsibility, not mine.

JOCELYN *suddenly sobs a little.*

(softening at once) I'm sorry. Sorry, Joss.

JOCELYN *(feebly tearful)* It's very hard sometimes.

NORRIS Yes, I know. I know it is. I'm sorry.

JOCELYN *rises to recover and, crossing to the table, starts to lay out five places.*

JOCELYN She's so...angry with me. I brought her up so lovingly. All the good things. Music. Painting. Beautiful books. She could have done anything she wanted. Danced. Played the piano. Sculpted. She's had pottery classes, acting lessons, everything.

NORRIS Sometimes it doesn't quite work out like that, does it?

JOCELYN How do you mean?

NORRIS *(cautiously)* I mean, maybe you should have tried her with – I don't know – panel-beating classes or something.

JOCELYN *(dismissing this)* Oh, Norris. She doesn't even have any friends. And she never even speaks to me now. I don't know what it is I've done.

There is a knocking on the front door.

Oh, thank heavens. He's back. Why does he never take his key? *(She opens the front door)*

BRINTON *is blown in.*

Brinton, are you wet? If so, dry your hair immediately.

BRINTON *(angrily)* I would like it known that my studio is now totally underwater. My canvases are actually floating off the floor. This, of course, is because the roof leaks.

JOCELYN I'll get you a towel.

JOCELYN *exits to the kitchen.*

BRINTON And why does the roof leak? Because I am not given money to repair it. I have been asking for money for three years.

NORRIS *(closing his eyes)* Oh, God.

BRINTON *(warming to his subject)* Let's feel the piano, shall we? *(He does so)* Oh, yes, nice and dry. Super. Well, the musical department's all right, isn't it? Let's feel the books, shall we? *(He moves to the bookcase)* See if they're damp. *(He feels the books)* No. No. Good news, everyone, the books are dry. It appears it's just the visual arts that are under water. Surprise, surprise.

NORRIS Look, give it a rest, will you, Brinton?

BRINTON Even the detective service seems to be nice and warm.

NORRIS Oh, Lord, save us.

BRINTON Don't you use that tone. You tell me how I'm supposed to paint in a flooded studio.

NORRIS Water colours. *(He laughs)* Water colours.

BRINTON *(looking at him contemptuously)* Mortimer was right. You are, you're a – whatever he said – a fizzy...thing.

NORRIS Probably.

JOCELYN *returns with a hand towel.*

BRINTON He's a tight-fisted bastard who doesn't give a damn about any of us, but he was right about you.

JOCELYN Here you are, Brin. Dry your hair before you catch cold.

BRINTON You help me, then.

JOCELYN Oh, honestly, Brin, you're forty whatever it is now. Really.

JOCELYN *stands behind* **BRINTON** *holding the back edge of the towel.* **BRINTON** *holds the front. They seesaw the towel to and fro across his scalp.*

BRINTON *(as they do this)* I'm forty-two and I don't see what difference that makes at all. I also have a coloured hippopotamus in my bath that swims, and squeaky soap.

NORRIS I know you do and I wish you'd take it out so that other people do not sit on it.

BRINTON Oh, it was you, was it?

NORRIS A nasty sharp little hippo.

BRINTON He is now, you've broken his flipper.

NORRIS Good.

JOCELYN I didn't know hippos had flippers. *(She finishes the task)* There. Dry.

BRINTON *(combing his hair with his fingers)* Yes.

AMY *enters with a final tray of tea things including the teapot and a cake.*

Ah. Teatime, is it?

JOCELYN Well done, darling, well done. Sorry, I meant to help you.

AMY *bangs the tea things down but does not reply. The telephone tings again. They all look up.*

Oh, he's finished.

NORRIS Been on for ages.

JOCELYN Would you see if Uncle Mortimer wants some tea, Amy?

AMY *goes towards the study.*

Ask him if he'd prefer it in there.

AMY *goes out.*

NORRIS Hopefully.

JOCELYN Do you want your tea by the fire, Norrie?

NORRIS If he's sitting at the table, yes.

JOCELYN You promised to apologize.

NORRIS All right.

BRINTON Is this cake any good?

JOCELYN I don't know, Amy bought it.

BRINTON *(studying the cake suspiciously)* Did he tell you my studio roof was leaking?

NORRIS *groans.*

JOCELYN Yes, Brinton, yes. *(She starts pouring the tea)* Maybe we could get you some polythene. That's not expensive.

BRINTON Polythene?

JOCELYN To spread over the roof.

BRINTON What, all over it?

JOCELYN Yes.

BRINTON It would be like painting inside a polythene bag.

JOCELYN No, it wouldn't.

BRINTON I'd suffocate.

JOCELYN Only over the roof.

BRINTON I'm not sitting all day in a polythene bag.

NORRIS *(muttering)* I wish you would.

BRINTON *looks at* **NORRIS** *nastily.*

AMY *slops back in from the study.*

JOCELYN Does he want it in there?

AMY He's coming in.

JOCELYN Oh.

BRINTON Good. I can have a word with him about my roof.

JOCELYN I wouldn't, Brinton. Not this evening. Pass that to Uncle Norrie, would you, Amy?

JOCELYN *hands* **AMY** *a cup.* **AMY** *clumps across to* **NORRIS. JOCELYN** *pours tea for* **BRINTON, AMY** *and herself and puts out these cups.* **AMY** *hands* **NORRIS** *his tea. He inspects it.* **AMY** *clumps back to the table.*

NORRIS Hey.

AMY What?

NORRIS You've left a bit in the cup.

AMY *(mirthlessly)* Ha-ha-ha-ha.

JOCELYN *looks anxiously at them both.* **AMY** *sits.* **NORRIS** *transfers his tea back from the saucer to the cup.*

BRINTON *(to* **AMY***)* Is this cake any good?

AMY No, it's foul. It's full of greasy fat. White sugar. Carbohydrates. Cholesterol and revolting processed sticky gunk that rots your brain and eats away your stomach lining. It's called Angel's Vomit.

JOCELYN *(wearily)* Amy.

BRINTON Sounds pretty good. *(He takes a piece of cake)*

AMY I'm having three pieces.

JOCELYN You're getting quite tubby, you know.

BRINTON *eats a mouthful of cake.*

BRINTON It's good. What do you call it again?

JOCELYN *(swiftly, before* **AMY** *can reply)* You want a piece, Norrie?

NORRIS No, no. Thank you. *(He pats his stomach)* I'll wait for my supper.

Silence.

JOCELYN Oh, it's Monday. Card night, isn't it?

Pause.

Are we going to play cards tonight?

Pause.

I'd like to. Are you going to play cards, Brinton?

BRINTON I keep losing.

JOCELYN No, you don't.

BRINTON I lost last week. I hate losing all the time.

JOCELYN It's only a game. It's only for matchsticks.

BRINTON *(angrily)* I don't happen to like losing matchsticks.

JOCELYN Norrie, are you playing?

NORRIS If everyone else is.

JOCELYN Amy and I are, aren't we, Amy?

AMY *doesn't reply.*

I wonder if Mortimer will.

In the distance, in the direction of the study, a door slams. They look towards the sound.

(softly) He's coming.

In a second **MORTIMER** *enters. He carries a statuette. It is his Timothy White and Taylor's Young Composer of the Year Award, 1966.*

During the following, **MORTIMER** *places the award on the piano. He then comes and sits at his place at the head of the table.*

Oh, your award. That's nice. Yes, it looks good there, Mortimer. See that, Amy? Uncle Mortimer's Award. Young Composer of the Year, wasn't it?

NORRIS *(softly)* For 1847.

MORTIMER *glares briefly at* **NORRIS**. *Silence.*

JOCELYN *(pouring a cup of tea for* **MORTIMER***)* A cup of tea, Mortimer?

MORTIMER *grunts.*

(sotto voce) Amy, offer Uncle Mortimer a piece of cake.

AMY *proffers the cake.* **MORTIMER** *glares at it.* **AMY** *slams the plate down again.* **BRINTON** *coughs nervously.*

(prattling brightly) We thought we'd all play cards after tea, Mortimer, seeing it's Monday. Would you like to play?

Pause.

It was very exciting last week. *(She looks over towards* **NORRIS** *and grimaces to him to speak)*

NORRIS *chooses to ignore her.*

Or would you prefer Scrabble? We haven't played Scrabble for donkey's years. *(Another look at* **NORRIS***)* Or Monopoly even.

There is a pause.

(under her breath) Norris.

NORRIS *(sighing and clearing his throat; about to apologize)* I—

MORTIMER Listen, you pack of numbskulls. I have something to say to you all. I want you to know that your combined behaviour a few minutes ago is never going to be forgotten.

JOCELYN Mortimer, we—

MORTIMER *(yelling)* Shut up!

Silence.

NORRIS *(quietly)* You speak to Jocelyn like that again, you are a dead man.

BRINTON *coughs.*

MORTIMER *(apparently unruffled)* I have no doubt in my own mind as to who was the ringleader. For ten years, he's been plotting to stifle my creative functions through a campaign of insidious sabotage.

JOCELYN *opens her mouth to speak but thinks better of it.*

Now, I have two things to say to you lot. You refuse to listen to my music so perhaps you'll listen to my words since they do have a direct bearing on all your futures. *(He looks round)* Listening now, are we? Firstly. Whoever it is who's been stealing money from my desk drawer had better stop.

JOCELYN Nobody's stealing, Mortimer—

MORTIMER So far, whoever you are, you've had a total of eighty-eight pounds, fifty-seven pence. Well, that's your lot. Any more and I'm calling the police in. They can handle it. All right? Point number two. As you are aware, when Mother died, this house, the contents of this house, all investments, securities, remaining capital, all of it passed to me. In line with Father's wishes. To dispose of, in due course, as I thought fit. Well, I'm pleased to tell you I am about to dispose of it – as I think fit.

There is a pause. **BRINTON** *coughs.*

JOCELYN What are you saying?

MORTIMER I'm leaving everything elsewhere. I thought you'd like to know.

There is a silence.

JOCELYN Everything?

MORTIMER Everything. So on my death, finis. Finito for you lot as well. You'll have no roof, no money, nothing. How does that appeal to you?

BRINTON You... *(He coughs)* ...can't do that.

MORTIMER Signed and sealed, locked in the solicitor's safe.

JOCELYN No, Mortimer, you can't.

NORRIS Don't worry, you can contest the will. He's got to be of sound mind before it's legal. You've got a very strong case.

MORTIMER *(viciously)* You shut up, you. You're not family. You're nothing. You're here under sufferance. So keep your mouth shut.

JOCELYN Mortimer, let me make it quite clear Norris is not here under sufferance. He is here because of me. You have no right to talk to him like that. He is family. He lives with me. And, as such—

MORTIMER Why don't you marry him, then? Make a proper job of it, Jossy. Second time lucky, eh?

NORRIS *(rising)* That's it... That's it, then!

JOCELYN It's all right, Norris.

NORRIS *sits back, glaring.* **MORTIMER** *returns the look.*

BRINTON May we ask why you're doing this to us?

MORTIMER I just think it's high time we broke up this little artistic colony, don't you? Wonderful idea, in theory. Dear Mother, full of useless ideals.

BRINTON *(incensed)* They were not useless. Nothing Mother ever did was useless.

MORTIMER She had you, didn't she?

BRINTON Why is he saying this to me? Why is he saying this to me?

JOCELYN Brinton.

MORTIMER It's been a washout, let's face it. Once I've gone, what are we left with? A painter who can't paint. A writer who can't write and a fifteen stone lump of a girl who can't do anything except stuff herself with cake.

BRINTON What do you mean? Can't paint? *(He coughs)* / Don't you tell me I can't paint. I can paint, don't you worry about that. I can paint.

MORTIMER We've only got your word for that, haven't we, laddie? Well, all I can say is that in thirty years, nobody's ever seen a bloody picture.

BRINTON } *(together)* { *(practically choking)* I'm...I'm working on it. Look who's talking. You can talk. Just because I'm a perfectionist.
JOCELYN } This is not fair, Mortimer. You mustn't do this to Brinton.

MORTIMER I can. I can talk. You go into my study. It's piled to the ceiling, my work. Eight symphonies. Four piano concertos. Two cello concertos. A violin concerto. A concerto for violin, oboe and bassoon. Three operas. Two oratorios. Seven string quartets. Two octets. A nonet. Ten string serenades—

BRINTON *(shouting him down)* And nobody's ever played any of them.

JOCELYN *(loudly)* All right, all right, all right, all right.

MORTIMER Well, let's see what you've got to show for it, eh, Brinton? What have you got to show for thirty years' artistic endeavour? Come on, Brinton, let's have a look at them. Wheel out those canvases. Let's have a really good viewing, shall we? How about it?

BRINTON *does not reply but merely coughs to himself.*

(picking up his award) The Timothy White and Taylor's Young Composer of the Year, 1966. To Mortimer Chalke. My case rests.

There is a brief pause.

AMY *(unexpectedly)* Who are you leaving it to, then?

MORTIMER *(startled)* Eh?

AMY All this? Anyone we know?

MORTIMER You won't. These two might remember her.

JOCELYN Her? Who?

MORTIMER Wendy Jones.

BRINTON *coughs.* **JOCELYN** *looks blank.*

He remembers her.

JOCELYN I can't say I... Oh! You mean that little girl? *That* little girl.

MORTIMER My student, Wendy Jones. My only student.

JOCELYN That little girl from the village?

MORTIMER Not a little girl now. It was twenty years ago.

JOCELYN Does she still live round here?

MORTIMER No. She moved south when she married. To Redhill. Married with three children. Twenty years ago she came to me and asked for piano lessons. Six months she came and I haven't seen her since. She showed great promise. Great promise. I don't even know if she still plays but she was my student and I want her to have all this. I've no children of my own so I'm leaving it to little Wendy.

JOCELYN This is ridiculous. She's a complete stranger. We shall contest this.

MORTIMER You can have a go.

JOCELYN She... She'll never agree anyway. She wouldn't agree to that. Disinheriting us. Throwing us out of our family home.

MORTIMER You'd be surprised what people will agree to when money's mentioned.

NORRIS He's mad, I've told you. He's howling.

JOCELYN She'd never agree.

MORTIMER She's interested enough to come up here anyway.

BRINTON *(alarmed)* Here?

MORTIMER I've invited her for a weekend. To talk about it. She'll be here in a fortnight to look it all over. You can ask her yourself.

BRINTON *(coughing)* She's coming here?

MORTIMER I've just phoned her. She sounded interested. So did her husband.

There is a slight pause.

JOCELYN *(tight-lipped)* It's *a fait accompli,* apparently.

MORTIMER I know you'd all love to see me dead but consider it. With this new will, it'll be in all your interests to keep me alive and happy, don't you think? *(He rises)* The way I look at it, it's a form of life insurance. *(He moves back towards the study, taking his award with him)*

NORRIS Mortimer?

MORTIMER *(mock-politely)* Norris.

NORRIS How did you ever come to trace this woman? Eh?

MORTIMER How do you think, Norris? I hired a private detective. A decent one. *(He laughs)*

MORTIMER *exits.*

There is a silence. **NORRIS** *rises and starts to move towards the study door.*

JOCELYN Norrie, where are you going?

NORRIS I think I'm probably going to strangle him. I could club him to death with a music stand but I think, on the whole, I'll strangle him.

JOCELYN *(rising and intercepting* **NORRIS***)* Norrie, no, no.

NORRIS That is the final blow, Jossy.

JOCELYN Kill him and we'll be no better off.

JOCELYN *seats* **NORRIS** *at the table; he allows her to do this.*

NORRIS Somebody's got to do it. For humanity.

Under the next, **AMY** *rises and goes to the sideboard. From a drawer, she takes out a pack of well-used cards and several labelled matchboxes, each with a name on it, containing matchstick "chips".*

JOCELYN He can't really do this to us, can he, Norrie? Leave it all to her?

BRINTON *(murmuring)* Wendy Jones.

JOCELYN You all right, Brin?

BRINTON *(coughing)* Yes.

JOCELYN *(to* **NORRIS***)* Can he do this to us?

NORRIS He's within his rights. Perfectly legal. You heard him. It's with the solicitors.

BRINTON Wendy Jones.

JOCELYN Well, what are we going to do? Anybody?

AMY Play cards?

NORRIS That's the sort of bright remark we expect from you, isn't it?

JOCELYN *(intercepting swiftly)* No, she's quite right, Norrie. That's what we must do. Carry on as normal. After all, he'll live for years.

NORRIS Is that a threat?

JOCELYN Why are we worrying? He's...very fit. We'll have to keep him fit, that's all. *(Briskly)* Come on, everyone, let's play cards.

They all move to the table except for **NORRIS**, *who stands puzzled.* **AMY** *sorts out the matchboxes, placing the cards in the middle of the table.*

NORRIS *(thoughtfully)* No, the person who ought to be worried, if I were her, is that girl.

JOCELYN Oh, Norrie, come on.

NORRIS I mean she's what we term in the trade, vulnerable.

JOCELYN Norrie, please come on and play.

NORRIS No, not now. I'm sorry, leave me out. Not now. *(He moves away from them back to the fireplace)*

JOCELYN *(frustratedly)* Oh.

BRINTON *(rising)* Nor me, I'm afraid.

JOCELYN *(sharply)* You sit down, Brinton, you're playing.

BRINTON *(without argument)* Righty-ho. *(He sits)*

JOCELYN Poker or pontoon?

AMY Pontoon.

JOCELYN Good. I'm banker then.

AMY Why?

JOCELYN Because I am.

BRINTON *(emptying his matchbox)* Somebody's been stealing my chips.

JOCELYN Rubbish.

BRINTON They have. I had thirty matches last week. Now I've only got ten.

JOCELYN You're worse than Mortimer, you are. Stealing money from his desk. Nobody here'd steal money.

There is a pause.

Would they?

BRINTON *(guiltily)* No. *(He coughs)*

JOCELYN Probably slipped down the back of the drawer. Right, here we go.

NORRIS *(pensively, to himself)* I wouldn't want to be in her shoes.

AMY What?

JOCELYN *(softly to her)* Leave him, Amy. *(She deals a card to each of them including herself)*

BRINTON *(as* **JOCELYN** *deals)* What happens when this girl comes? What are we going to do? What are we going to say to Wendy Jones?

JOCELYN Well. We'll— *(She lifts her card by the corner to take a secret look)*

The others look at their cards likewise.

– place your bets – when she comes, we'll have to be very, very nice to her indeed, won't we?

BRINTON Yes.

AMY Yes.

NORRIS *(half to himself)* If this was a different family altogether I reckon she could be in a spot of trouble.

They place their bets; as they do so, they look at each other momentarily. **JOCELYN** *starts to deal the second card to each of them.*

The lights fade to blackout.

Scene Two

The same. Saturday, early evening. Two weeks later.

The room has been tidied a little since we last saw it. The electric fire has gone and there is a real fire burning in the grate. There are six champagne glasses on a tray and a few bowls of cocktail nibbles laid out around the place. **NORRIS** *stands alone. He seems a little restless. He is dressed up more than he normally would be when he's away from work. (In fact everyone,* **JOCELYN, AMY** *and* **BRINTON**, *as they appear, will be seen to have made an effort. All with varying degrees of success)* **NORRIS** *looks at his watch.*

JOCELYN *enters upstairs and descends.*

NORRIS No sign.

JOCELYN They're dreadfully late. Perhaps her train was delayed. Yes. *(She looks out of the window briefly)* It's very bleak for her, Mother's room. I've done what I can to make it welcoming but it's very dreary, I'm afraid. It hasn't been used since she died. Ah well, done my best.

Pause.

NORRIS Look at this. *(He indicates the glasses and nibbles)* Look at this. He's really enjoying this, isn't he? Gloating. Did you know we were having champagne? All for her. He's laughing at us. That's what he's doing. Dancing on our graves before we're in them.

JOCELYN Well—

NORRIS Have you ever heard him so cheerful? Whistling about the place. Singing his bloody awful music. You notice he never sings anybody else's. And we're just standing here like stuffed...owls...to the slaughter. I mean, what have we got to celebrate? Eh?

JOCELYN Nothing much.

NORRIS Exactly.

Pause.

JOCELYN That chimney's smoking a bit.

NORRIS I'm not surprised. There hasn't been a fire in that grate for...five years. At least. Coal's too expensive, he says. I said to him, forget coal, what about wood, mate? Get a few logs in. They're cheap enough. You're the sort of person, he says, who's prepared to burn his own birthright. What a load of cobblers.

Pause.

I mean, what are we doing meeting this woman? I don't want to meet her.

JOCELYN You've only got to say hallo. We're going out soon, anyway.

NORRIS And that's another thing. Forcing us to go out. What right's he got to do that?

JOCELYN That's all right, we were all going out, anyway. Brinton's got his art meeting. Amy's got— *(She checks herself)* We all wanted to.

NORRIS I didn't want to go out tonight.

JOCELYN Yes, you did. You want to see the film as much as I do.

NORRIS Not necessarily tonight, I didn't. I don't necessarily want to go out tonight. I resent being told when to go out. I might have wanted to go out another night for all he knew.

JOCELYN Well, you can't. It's the last night tonight.

Pause.

That awful old car of his. He should have taken mine. Not that mine's much better.

Slight pause.

We haven't been to the cinema for ages, have we? Remember we used to go twice a week sometimes? I'm really looking forward to it. We should have gone to them all, you know. There's a whole season of them. These old thrillers. They've been on for weeks.

NORRIS At this rate, we're going to miss it anyway. *(He heads towards the stairs)*

JOCELYN Where are you going?

NORRIS I'm going to take off this tie.

JOCELYN Oh, Norris.

NORRIS Ridiculous getting dressed up like this. For some woman who's going to kick us all out on the street.

JOCELYN I say, if we're nice to her, she might—

AMY *appears on the stairs.*

NORRIS *stops as he nearly runs in to* **AMY**.

Oh, there you are.

AMY Yes.

JOCELYN What were you doing up there? You haven't been in my room?

AMY No, I bloody haven't.

JOCELYN *(with a look at* **NORRIS***)* All right.

NORRIS *hurries out.*

I like to know when you borrow things, that's all.

AMY What things?

JOCELYN You know.

AMY I borrowed a safety pin three years ago.

JOCELYN That wasn't all.

AMY What?

JOCELYN I said, that wasn't all you borrowed.

AMY I went up because I heard a noise.

JOCELYN What sort of noise?

AMY Bang. Crash.

JOCELYN Did you find out what it was?

AMY No.

JOCELYN Odd.

A pause. **AMY** *eats a few nibbles.*

Don't eat all those, Amy.

AMY Reserved for Madam, are they?

JOCELYN No, they're for all of us. When they get here. They shouldn't be long. Amy I'm off in a minute. We can give you a lift.

AMY No, I'll get the bus.

JOCELYN If you want to. What's it tonight? Saturday. It's your drama class, isn't it?

AMY Yes.

JOCELYN Are you still enjoying those?

AMY Great.

JOCELYN More than the dance classes?

AMY Yes.

JOCELYN Or the painting?

AMY Yes. *(She takes another handful of nibbles)*

JOCELYN Amy, will you stop eating those? *(She takes the bowl and moves it away from* **AMY***)* Apart from anything else, you're growing the size of a house.

AMY So?

Pause.

JOCELYN Did I tell you who I saw the other day? When I was shopping? Gwen Carter. *(Pause)* Remember her? Yes, of course you must do. She's doing the drama class as well, isn't she? *(Pause)* She says you haven't been for a year. Apparently you said something awful to the woman in charge and walked out after the first lesson.

AMY *is silent.*

What on earth have you been doing instead?

Silence.

You must have been going somewhere every Saturday evening. And on Tuesdays. Presumably you haven't been to dance class either?

Silence.

Amy, where have you been?

AMY I can do what I like with my own time. I'm old enough, now.

JOCELYN *(soothingly)* Yes, I know that. I'm not trying to... I mean, I just... I just wonder... I just was... I just was wondering why you've bothered to lie to us. To me.

AMY *(muttering)* I didn't want... I didn't... *(Pause)* I didn't...

JOCELYN *(waiting patiently; after a pause)* You didn't what?

AMY I didn't want to...to talk.

JOCELYN Talk? You didn't want to talk?

AMY We always talk about everything. Let's have a good talk about it. It's boring.

JOCELYN But where do you go to, then? Every Tuesday and Saturday?

AMY The café.

JOCELYN The café? What café?

AMY At the bus station.

JOCELYN What, all evening? What a dreadful way to spend the evening. It's not a very pleasant place, is it? I seem to remember. It has that awful music playing all the time. What do you do in there? Are you meeting someone?

AMY No.

JOCELYN What, then?

AMY Just eat.

JOCELYN Eat?

AMY Yes.

JOCELYN On your own? What, all evening? What on earth do you eat?

AMY Food.

JOCELYN *(irritably)* I know food, but—

AMY Eggs, beans, chips. Hamburgers. Fish and chips. Sausage and chips. Steak pie and chips. Apple pie and ice cream. Chocolate gâteau—

JOCELYN *(appalled)* My God. Why?

AMY I'm hungry.

JOCELYN It must cost a fortune. Where on earth do you get the—? *(She checks herself)* Is that where you'll go tonight?

AMY Probably.

JOCELYN Amy, something's awfully wrong, isn't it? I mean, there's... I mean, it seems to me you're bottling, darling, you're bottling. It's all in there, isn't it? Bottled. Amy you've simply got to learn to uncork, somehow. If only you'd paint or write or – I don't know – sing, even. Let it all out. *(Pause)* Well, at least let us give you a lift in. We'll drop you at the... bus station. Amy, would it...would it help if you went away for a little? I don't want you to, don't get me wrong. I love having you here with me, you know I do. But maybe you need a change. Somewhere new for a while.

AMY I couldn't leave. I couldn't leave you here.

JOCELYN Me?

AMY Not alone with him.

JOCELYN Him? You mean Uncle Norris?

AMY I couldn't leave you with him. He's useless. They're all useless. I couldn't leave you with them.

JOCELYN *(rather taken aback)* I... I didn't realize you felt like that.

AMY I couldn't leave.

JOCELYN Well, I'm very touched. Thank you. *(She flaps her arms a little as if considering whether or not to embrace* **AMY**. *She decides against it and nibbles a crisp instead; half to herself)* Very touched. Thank you. *(She passes* **AMY** *a crisp rather absentmindedly)*

AMY *takes the crisp. They both nibble in silence.*

There is a knock on the front door.

Oh, heavens, it's them. *(She hurries to the front door and turns before she opens it)* All right? Here we go, then. Big smile, darling.

AMY *smiles.* **JOCELYN** *opens the door.*

BRINTON *enters.*

BRINTON Thank you.

JOCELYN Brinton, will you please remember your key? Every time.

BRINTON Don't blame me. Someone's stolen it.

JOCELYN *(closing the door)* You've lost it.

BRINTON No, I haven't.

JOCELYN You've lost nine to my knowledge.

BRINTON I have not lost nine. *(To* **AMY***)* Have I? I haven't lost nine.

AMY *(contemptuously)* You're useless.

AMY *exits to the kitchen.*

BRINTON She's extremely rude to me, your daughter. She really is. I don't know why. I'm always very polite to her.

Pause.

I think it's going to rain again. My studio's only just dried out from the last time.

JOCELYN *(glancing at her watch)* They're taking a long time.

BRINTON I don't know how I'm going to go through all this. I really don't.

JOCELYN *(looking at him, concerned)* Are you all right?

BRINTON No, I am not all right. *(He coughs)* I'm saying I am not at all all right, I'm not all right at all. How am I going to face this girl? How?

JOCELYN Wendy?

BRINTON What am I going to say to her?

JOCELYN Brin, how well did you know her, then? Before?

BRINTON Every inch of her.

JOCELYN How extraordinary. I didn't know you'd even spoken to her, Brin.

BRINTON I haven't. I've never spoken to her. Well, I said hallo, I think. Once. Hi! But she didn't say hallo. She never spoke.

I never heard her voice. I've imagined it a lot but I never heard it. Because of the window.

JOCELYN Brin, what are you talking about?

BRINTON But then she was a very quiet girl, wasn't she? So still. Serene. Shy, even. She used to sit here at the piano, she... she arrived in the summer. I remember that. It was before Mother had my studio built and I used to sit on the lawn out there. That's when there was a lawn out there. And I could see her through the window. Practising this piano. And I'd watch her listening to Mortimer rabbiting away, waving his arms... And sometimes, very occasionally, I'd see her smile. And at those moments, she became the most perfect, the most beautiful vision I'd ever seen in my life. That long fine hair and that pale, innocent face. Breathtaking. Each day she came after that, I'd sit out there – pretending to sketch flowers or trees – but I only drew her. She's all I've ever drawn or painted since. Versions of her. But I've never got anywhere near. Caught that beauty. Nowhere. Not in twenty years. It's an awfully long time to hold a vision, isn't it? Twenty years.

JOCELYN *(affected)* Oh, Brin. That's really moving.

BRINTON Dreadful.

JOCELYN So romantic. How lovely. And it's been a secret all these years?

BRINTON What am I going to do, Joss? What's going to happen to me?

JOCELYN *(shaking her head)* To any of us.

BRINTON *peers out through the curtain.*

BRINTON Oh.

JOCELYN What is it?

BRINTON I think there's someone out there. By the front door.

JOCELYN Who?

BRINTON I can't really see. It's terribly dark. We never got that porch light mended, did we? *(In despair)* If only I'd been born an electrician. Or a roofing mender.

JOCELYN *(going to look)* It must be them.

NORRIS *enters on the stairs.*

JOCELYN Norris, they're here. *(Calling)* Amy!

NORRIS About time.

JOCELYN *(calling)* Amy!

AMY *enters from the kitchen.*

There is a rather mild knocking on the front door.

There they are now.

NORRIS Why doesn't he open it then?

BRINTON Perhaps he's lost his key.

JOCELYN Amy, open the door.

AMY Why me?

JOCELYN Because... Because I can't. Now remember, everyone, nice as you can.

NORRIS It's not going to make a scrap of difference, Joss, however nice we are. If she wants the house, she's going to have it.

JOCELYN She... At least, she can see we're nice.

AMY *(standing, holding the door)* Excuse me, do you want me to open this door or not?

JOCELYN If she sees how happy we all are here, as a family, she may...have second thoughts—

AMY Excuse me.

JOCELYN ...about turning us out.

NORRIS Look, she's got three kids and a husband. She's got the chance of inheriting a free house and a small fortune. She's hardly going to say no, is she?

There is more knocking on the door.

JOCELYN We don't know. She might.

AMY Right, I'm opening the door.

NORRIS It's human nature, Joss, human nature. Come down out of the clouds.

AMY Here I go.

JOCELYN Yes, yes. Open the door! Open the door!

JOCELYN *braces herself expectantly.* **BRINTON** *backs away in apprehension to the foot of the stairs. He coughs.* **AMY** *opens the door.*

There is a pause.

Then, very slowly and nervously, out of the darkness, steps **WENDY WINDWOOD** *née Jones. She steps cautiously inside. The years have wrought drastic changes upon the ethereal child described by* **BRINTON**. *Instead stands a cosy, pleasant, rather shy, middle-aged mum, at present a little dishevelled and travel-worn. She smiles. Her smile is her main protection against strangers and becomes a more or less permanent fixture whenever she is in company. She holds a small vanity case.*

WENDY Hallo. Wendy Windwood. Sorry I'm late.

JOCELYN Hallo.

NORRIS Hallo.

AMY 'llo.

WENDY *looks naturally towards* **BRINTON** *as the one who has not spoken. He is staring at her with an expression which somewhat approaches horror. Somewhere,* *suddenly, from deep within him comes a low wail of despair which slowly increases in volume and pitch. It is the sound of a man's lifelong image shattering. Still moaning, he turns and plunges headlong up the stairs.*

BRINTON *exits. His voice fades away.*

Silence. **WENDY** *looks a little nervous.*

JOCELYN I'm sorry. That's my Brinton brother. Brother Brinton. You remember my brother Brinton?

WENDY Oh, yes, yes.

JOCELYN I'm Jocelyn, of course. Brinton's a little, a little—

NORRIS Mad.

JOCELYN Excitable. He... This is my...my friend... My very, very good friend, Norris. Norris Honeywell. Norris, this is Wendy - now, it's not Jones any more, is it? It's - now, let's get it right - Wendy Woodwind.

WENDY Windwood.

JOCELYN Wendy Windwood, yes. Sorry.

NORRIS How do you do?

JOCELYN This is my daughter, Amy.

WENDY Oh, how do you do? Your daughter. That's nice.

AMY *shakes hands with* **WENDY** *rather listlessly.*

(looking towards **NORRIS***)* Yes, I can see who she takes after.

NORRIS No, she's not my daughter. She's her daughter.

JOCELYN My daughter.

WENDY Yes, yes. Amy. It's a lovely name, Amy. We were going to have an Amy.

JOCELYN Oh, why didn't you?

WENDY They're all boys.

JOCELYN Boys?

WENDY Three boys, yes. Gary, Graham and Gilbert. All the Gs. *(She laughs)*

JOCELYN Gracious. Actually, Amy's really Amaryllis but we shortened it.

WENDY Oh, yes. Well. Yes. Amaryllis, that's unusual. Where did you get that from?

AMY Mozart.

WENDY Pardon?

AMY I'm named after Mozart. Wolfgang Amaryllis Mozart.

WENDY *(mystified)* Oh.

JOCELYN *(rather sharply)* Close the door, please, Amy.

AMY *closes the front door.*

(to **WENDY***)* Mortimer is with you, isn't he? I thought he went to meet you.

WENDY Yes, he did. He...er... Would it be in order for me to sit down just for a moment? As a matter of fact, I'm just a little bit at threes and twos.

JOCELYN Yes, of course. Please. Please do. *(She proffers a chair by the table)* Or would you prefer an easy chair?

WENDY No, no. I just want to—

NORRIS *(assisting* **WENDY** *into the chair)* Here, allow me.

WENDY Thank you. *(She sits)*

JOCELYN Have you had a bad journey? Would you like some tea or water or—

WENDY Well, no. As a matter of fact, we had a little mishap on the way here.

JOCELYN Mishap?

WENDY Yes, it was nothing serious fortunately. Well, it could have been but luckily it didn't turn out that way.

NORRIS In the train?

WENDY No, in the car. You know the hill just before we get to your drive?

JOCELYN What, you mean Gadds Hill?

WENDY The steep one, yes. Just as we were coming down it, the brakes failed.

NORRIS Failed?

JOCELYN Oh, my God.

WENDY It was terrifying. We were coming down about seventy miles an hour.

JOCELYN Is my brother all right?

WENDY Yes. Oh, yes. He managed to turn the car into that little place at the bottom for runaways, you know.

JOCELYN Yes.

WENDY With the gravel. Then we... He drove it very slowly the rest of the way here.

JOCELYN Where is Mortimer now?

WENDY I left him at the bottom of your drive. He was having a look to see if he could see anything. Striking matches. He told me to come on up.

NORRIS I suppose I'd better lend a hand.

JOCELYN Yes, do, Norris. Thank you. See if he's all right, would you? Take him a torch. Amy, do you know where the torch is? I think Brinton lost it.

AMY Hang on.

NORRIS *exits through the front door.*

AMY *goes off towards the study.*

JOCELYN What a frightening thing to happen.

WENDY Couldn't be helped. Nobody's fault, was it?

JOCELYN No.

WENDY *(looking around her)* It's funny coming back. Twenty years.

JOCELYN Twenty years, is it? Well, it's probably all much the same.

WENDY *(seeing the piano)* Oh, look – I remember this. *(She moves over to it)*

JOCELYN You still play?

WENDY No. Not really, no.

JOCELYN Shame.

AMY *returns from the study, carrying a bicycle lamp.*

Oh, well found.

AMY Took it off his bike.

JOCELYN What, Brinton's bike?

AMY Yes.

JOCELYN Well, for heaven's sake remember to put it back. Or we'll never hear the end of it.

AMY *goes out of the front door, leaving it ajar behind her.*

WENDY We've only got quite a small flat at present. Just over the shop.

JOCELYN You've got a shop?

WENDY Yes. A little pet shop. It belongs to us both, of course. But I run it. My husband's got the newsagent's just round the corner. So we're both kept very busy.

JOCELYN How exciting.

WENDY My sister-in-law's looking after WendyPets just for the weekend.

JOCELYN Very busy for you.

WENDY Oh, yes. Well, you have to keep going, don't you? *(She looks around again)* No, I don't think it's changed that much really. Still got the same wallpaper by the look of it. *(She laughs)*

JOCELYN *(laughing, too)* Yes, yes. Probably.

> **WENDY** *moves round the room, absently feeling for dust and giving the impression of inspecting the fixtures and fittings.*

WENDY Yes, yes. Yes.

> **JOCELYN** *watches her with a slight frown of irritation.*

JOCELYN *(laughing)* See anything you fancy?

WENDY Sorry? *(She laughs)* Oh, yes, sorry. I'm terrible.

JOCELYN Look, would you...like to come upstairs? See your room? Wash your hands?

WENDY Yes. Lovely, yes. I'm a little bit sticky. Trains are always that little bit sticky, aren't they? Have you noticed? On your hands?

JOCELYN No, I can't say I have. It depends where you put them, I suppose. *(She picks up* **WENDY***'s little case)* Is this all your luggage or have you—?

WENDY No, there's another big one in the car.

JOCELYN Oh, we'll bring that in, don't worry.

> **AMY** *enters through the front door with* **WENDY***'s larger matching suitcase.*

Yes, look. Splendid. Here we are. Thank you, Amy, I'll take it.

WENDY Thank you.

AMY *hands the case to* **JOCELYN** *and goes immediately towards the kitchen.*

JOCELYN Have they found anything wrong? With the car?

AMY Don't ask me.

AMY *exits.*

JOCELYN *(smiling apologetically to* **WENDY***)* Teenagers. *(She starts up the stairs)*

WENDY *(following* **JOCELYN***)* Don't tell me. Can you manage that?

JOCELYN Fine. How old are yours?

WENDY Fourteen, eleven and nine.

JOCELYN Heavens.

WENDY *(pointing upward)* You've got a little damp coming in there, did you know?

JOCELYN Yes. So we have. Never mind. All part of life's rich texture, isn't it?

They continue on up the stairs.

MORTIMER *enters, removing his overcoat.*

Did you find anything, Mortimer?

MORTIMER I didn't. I don't even know where the brakes are kept. Norris is looking. He may be able to tell us.

JOCELYN Terrifying. I'm just showing Mrs Windwood upstairs.

WENDY Wendy.

JOCELYN Wendy.

MORTIMER Well, come down soon. We'll have a drink.

WENDY Wonderful.

JOCELYN *and* **WENDY** *head off.*

JOCELYN *(as they go)* You're only at the top of the stairs here. It's Mother's old room. I hope you'll find it comfortable...

JOCELYN *and* **WENDY** *go off.*

MORTIMER *stares after them for a second, then, humming to himself he takes a piece of paper from his pocket, consults it briefly, replaces it in his pocket and then heads towards his study, removing his coat and scarf. For some unaccountable reason, as he does so he laughs.*

He exits.

A second later, **NORRIS** *comes in the front door, carrying the cycle lamp. He switches off the lamp and closes the door behind him. He puts the lamp down on a side table. He looks thoughtful.*

MORTIMER *enters from the study.*

MORTIMER Find anything?

NORRIS *(grimly)* Yes, I did.

MORTIMER What do I do, then? Sue the garage?

NORRIS I don't want to cause a panic but it is my professional opinion that those brakes were tampered with.

MORTIMER Tampered?

NORRIS The connections had been loosened in two places. From the look of it, done within the last twenty-four hours and in a hurry. With either a wrench or an adjustable spanner.

MORTIMER What are you talking about?

NORRIS Marks on the metal. Fresh, you see. Newly made. Hadn't had time to get dirty.

MORTIMER Norris, you're not only inept, you're potty.

NORRIS You don't believe me?

MORTIMER Of course I don't believe you. Tampering with the brakes. Come on, think of something original. If you want to invent a detective story, let's have a bit of imagination. What about cyanide in the steering column or something. As I turn sharp left, it releases a deadly cloud of poisonous gas. *(He starts towards the kitchen)*

NORRIS Listen, I know what I'm talking about, Chalke.

MORTIMER What about a black mamba in the glove compartment? That's a good one.

NORRIS It's for your own protection I'm telling you this. Personally, I wouldn't give a stuff if you fell head first down a mine shaft.

MORTIMER Oh, do go away.

JOCELYN *appears on the stairs.*

JOCELYN What are you arguing about now?

MORTIMER No arguments, Joss.

NORRIS No.

JOCELYN You could have fooled me. Did the brakes just fail? Just like that? No prior warning at all?

MORTIMER No. We stopped for a moment on the way back while I popped in to see dear old Annie—

JOCELYN Old Annie? What, you mean our old Annie? What for?

MORTIMER Oh, I'd promised her some magazines ages ago. I've been carting them round in the car meaning to give them to her. Kept forgetting.

JOCELYN She's only a couple of hundred yards away. I could have taken them.

MORTIMER I restarted the car, off we went, down Gadds Hill, suddenly couldn't stop.

NORRIS Did you leave the car unattended at all?

MORTIMER No. Wendy stayed in it.

JOCELYN Why unattended?

MORTIMER *(with a look at* **NORRIS***)* It doesn't matter.

JOCELYN You don't think someone could have...?

MORTIMER No, we don't think anything of the kind, do we, Norris? Do we?

NORRIS *(reluctantly)* No, no, no.

MORTIMER I'll get the champagne.

MORTIMER *exits into the kitchen.*

JOCELYN What's going on?

NORRIS *(excitedly)* Look, I have to tell you, Joss. I have to. The most fantastic thing. You're not going to believe it. The fact is that—

From upstairs there is a scream from **WENDY***, followed by a crash.*

JOCELYN What on earth was that?

NORRIS *(springing into action)* Don't panic, don't panic! Stay there! *(He hurries up the stairs)* Don't, whatever you do, move. Stay there!

NORRIS *goes off upstairs.*

AMY *comes out of the kitchen.*

AMY What was that?

NORRIS *(offstage)* Stay there!

JOCELYN No idea.

From offstage, there comes the sound of **NORRIS** *hammering and banging on the bedroom door.*

Do you think we ought to see? *(She moves towards the stairs)*

AMY *follows* **JOCELYN**.

MORTIMER *comes out of the kitchen with a champagne bottle which he is in the process of opening.*

MORTIMER What's all that din?

JOCELYN Wendy seems to have had an accident. Norris is seeing to it.

MORTIMER *(sarcastically)* Oh, wonderful.

JOCELYN *and* **AMY** *head up the stairs.*

NORRIS *enters and comes thundering down the stairs past them.*

JOCELYN What's happening?

NORRIS Her door's jammed. Something's blocking the door. *(He crosses to the front door and opens it)*

MORTIMER Where are you going, then?

NORRIS I'm going to try to get in the window.

NORRIS *goes out of the front door.*

JOCELYN *hurries downstairs to follow* **NORRIS**.

AMY *exits upstairs.*

JOCELYN *(calling after* **NORRIS***)* There's a ladder round the back somewhere. There should be.

JOCELYN *exits.*

From upstairs, the sound of **WENDY**'s *faint voice can be heard.*

WENDY *(offstage, distant)* Help. Help.

MORTIMER *puts down the champagne bottle. He whistles to himself a little.*

BRINTON *appears, rather blearily, on the landing.*

BRINTON What's happening?

MORTIMER I don't know. Where have you been?

BRINTON Lying down. On my bed. I felt a little...weak.

MORTIMER How unusual.

BRINTON Hell of a noise. It woke me up.

JOCELYN *comes in the front door, rather breathless.*

MORTIMER Now what?

JOCELYN *(crossing the room and going straight up the stairs)* Norris is reaching her by ladder. Luckily one just under her window. *(She tries to dodge round* **BRINTON***)* Oh, do get out of the way, Brinton.

BRINTON Sorry.

JOCELYN Sorry. Something seems to have fallen on her.

JOCELYN *goes off upstairs.*

BRINTON *(coming downstairs)* I wish I knew what was going on.

MORTIMER Don't worry. All's well. Honeywell's at the helm. *(He crosses to the front door)* I wish to God they'd keep this door shut. You spend a fortune trying to heat the room.

MORTIMER *closes the front door and prepares to open the bottle of champagne.*

BRINTON *fiddles with the glasses.*

What are you doing?

BRINTON *(guiltily)* Nothing. *(He coughs)*

MORTIMER Well, leave them alone. They're very expensive, those glasses.

AMY *comes down the stairs.*

AMY The wardrobe fell on her and jammed the door.

MORTIMER Your grandmother's wardrobe?

AMY Yes.

MORTIMER It's huge.

BRINTON It is.

MORTIMER I thought it was screwed to the wall.

BRINTON It was. Screwed to the wall.

MORTIMER Ah well, must have come loose. Like everything else in this house. So long as Wendy's all right.

AMY Seems to be.

MORTIMER Good.

AMY *(with one her rare smiles)* Not having an awful lot of luck, is she?

BRINTON How do you mean?

AMY *(helping herself to some nibbles)* Quite a lot happening to her, don't you think?

BRINTON *(puzzled)* Oh, yes, yes. Are those nice?

AMY Disgusting.

BRINTON Ah. *(He helps himself to some)*

JOCELYN *comes downstairs supporting* **WENDY**.

JOCELYN Easy now, easy does it.

WENDY *(limping slightly)* Oh, dear, oh dear.

MORTIMER *(opening the champagne bottle)* Here we are. Now, are you all right, Wendy?

WENDY Oh, yes. Not too bad. Just caught my leg. Oh, look at this. Champagne, eh?

MORTIMER I think you've earned it, Wendy. It's been a positive obstacle course for you so far.

WENDY *(laughing)* Yes, yes.

JOCELYN It's just your leg, is it?

WENDY Yes, it's probably only a bruise. A little bruise. Lucky I saw it coming. I just jumped sideways.

MORTIMER *(as he pours the champagne)* We were just remarking that wardrobe always was potentially lethal. Don't you remember? It nearly fell on Mother once.

JOCELYN Goodness, so it did.

BRINTON Yes, yes. I was on top of it at the time. *(To* **WENDY***)* Hiding. From Mother.

MORTIMER So you were. That's why we had it screwed to the wall. It must have worked loose over the years. I'm terribly sorry.

WENDY Ah, well. Accidents happen. Nobody's fault.

JOCELYN No.

BRINTON No.

AMY No.

WENDY Mr Honeywell was marvellous. I didn't realize he was a detective.

JOCELYN Oh, yes.

WENDY Yes, he came through the window like one.

JOCELYN Here we are. Sit over here. It's the most comfortable.

JOCELYN *steers* **WENDY** *towards an easy chair.*

MORTIMER You want to hand these round, somebody? Amy?

AMY *starts to take round the glasses, beginning with* **WENDY**.

Norris is coming down, I take it? Or has it fallen on him as well?

JOCELYN No, he's coming. He's just crawling around looking for something.

WENDY I was just hanging up a skirt, you know, so it wouldn't crease. And I opened the wardrobe door and bang.

JOCELYN Terrible.

WENDY Not my day, is it? Should have stayed in bed, I think. *(She laughs)*

JOCELYN Yes.

NORRIS *enters upstairs and descends looking grim and thoughtful.*

NORRIS *(softly to* **MORTIMER***)* Could I have a word with you?

MORTIMER Not now, Norris, no.

NORRIS It's a matter of life and death.

MORTIMER *(putting down his glass)* Oh, for God's sake. *(To the others)* Excuse me.

NORRIS *leads* **MORTIMER** *to the landing.*

WENDY Chapter of accidents.

MORTIMER Well?

WENDY *(noticing* **BRINTON***, who has retreated to a corner)* Oh, hallo, there. We didn't really get a chance to say hallo before, did we?

NORRIS *(opening his palm to display six screws)* Look at these.

BRINTON No.

MORTIMER Screws, aren't they?

NORRIS Precisely. Screws that should have been in that wardrobe, but weren't.

WENDY Remember me then, do you?

BRINTON No. Yes.

MORTIMER Must have fallen out.

NORRIS Look at them, man.

WENDY Still doing the painting, are you?

BRINTON Yes. No.

NORRIS Notice anything odd about them?

WENDY That's the spirit.

MORTIMER No. One screw looks much like another to me.

NORRIS They were originally rawlplugged into the wall. You can see the holes.

MORTIMER Splendid.

NORRIS Very well, then. If they'd pulled away accidentally, the rawlplugs would have come with them. Or stayed in the wall. One or the other.

WENDY *decides to get out of her armchair; she rises and wobbles. During the following she walks to and fro testing her leg, assisted first by* **BRINTON** *and then* **JOCELYN**.

BRINTON *(as* **WENDY** *rises and wobbles)* Whoops, allow me. *(He takes* **WENDY***'s glass from her and puts it on the table)*

WENDY Thank you. *(She smiles at* **BRINTON***)*

BRINTON *smiles back.*

MORTIMER Yes. So?

NORRIS *(triumphantly)* Then tell me this. Where are the rawlplugs now, eh?

MORTIMER How the hell should I know?

NORRIS Don't you see the significance?

JOCELYN *(to* **WENDY***)* How is it?

WENDY Well, it's definitely only a bruise. Nothing broken.

JOCELYN Good.

WENDY *paces round the room.*

MORTIMER *(smiling)* I think you're perilously close to certification, Honeywell.

NORRIS *(shouting)* What's the matter with you people?

Everyone looks up at them, startled.

MORTIMER *(waving to them, reassuringly)* Nothing. Carry on. *(To* **NORRIS***)* Now, pull yourself together and have some champagne. *(He returns to the table and picks up* **WENDY***'s glass)*

NORRIS *(incredulously; to himself)* My God, what's the matter with the man?

MORTIMER Sorry, everyone. Now, where were we? *(To* **WENDY***)* How's the leg? Still working?

WENDY *(cheerily)* Just about.

MORTIMER Everyone got a glass, have they?

WENDY Oh. *(She looks around)* Where did I put mine?

MORTIMER Oh, I'm sorry, have I taken yours?

WENDY Don't worry. I haven't drunk from it.

JOCELYN Here's another. *(She hands* **WENDY** *a spare glass from the table)*

BRINTON That's mine.

JOCELYN Well, take another one.

BRINTON I don't want another one. I want that one. That's my one.

AMY Here. *(She thrusts a glass at* **BRINTON***)*

BRINTON *(distraught)* But I... I—

WENDY *(handing* **BRINTON** *the glass she is holding)* Here. Have this.

BRINTON and WENDY exchange glasses. BRINTON calms down.

JOCELYN Brinton, what do you say?

BRINTON *(sotto)* Thank you.

MORTIMER If we've all quite finished. If I may. This is simply just to welcome our guest, Wendy, whom we haven't seen for a very long time and to say—

WENDY Excuse me.

MORTIMER ...and to say—

WENDY Excuse me.

MORTIMER Wendy, I'm sorry.

WENDY Could I just... I just wanted to say – because I know you're all going out in a minute and maybe I won't get a chance to speak to you again...

Everyone looks at each other.

...all together like this. I just wanted to say that when Mr Chalke – Mortimer – phoned me offering us your wonderful gift of the house and everything, well, Ollie and I, that's my husband, we really were overwhelmed. I mean, it's really so generous of you. Even with death duties. And, well, it won't be for some long time yet, hopefully.

MORTIMER laughs heartily.

I'm sure it won't, hopefully. Nonetheless, one of the reasons I know Mr Chalke said you thought of us, me and my family – me and Ollie and Gary and Graham and Gilbert – one of the reasons was that you wanted to know that the house would remain the warm and friendly place it's always been. Well, I must tell you, besides our children, my husband and I have a dream that one day we will become full-scale breeders. Breeding King Charles spaniels, which are our favourites. We can think of no better place to do this than here in your house. And we'll do all in our power to keep it warm and friendly. Me and my family and the happy barking of contented dogs. Thank you.

There is a silence.

MORTIMER *applauds.*

MORTIMER Marvellous, Wendy.

WENDY *(shyly)* Thank you.

MORTIMER What more can I add? Happy dogs. *(He raises his glass)*

WENDY *(toasting him back)* Happy dogs.

EVERYONE *(muttering)* Happy dogs.

They drink. **MORTIMER** *almost instantly doubles up, choking and dropping his glass, spilling the contents on to the carpet.*

MOTIMER *(his hand to his mouth)* Aaaaggh! Aaaaggh!

NORRIS	*(together)*	What is it? What is it?
JOCELYN		Mortimer –
BRINTON		What's happening?
WENDY		What's the matter?
AMY		Are you all right?

MORTIMER *(rushing towards the kitchen, choking)* It's burning. It's burning me.

MORTIMER *exits.*

The others stand transfixed.

WENDY *(finally)* Do you think we should do something?

JOCELYN Yes, yes. I'll see, I'll see.

JOCELYN *goes out to the kitchen.*

BRINTON *(bending to pick up* **MORTIMER**'s *glass)* I think it must have been something in the glass—

NORRIS *(sharply)* Don't, whatever you do, touch that glass.

BRINTON *(startled)* What?

NORRIS *(calmer)* Don't touch the glass, Brinton, there's a good chap.

BRINTON *(puzzled)* Righto. *(He leaves the glass)*

NORRIS *removes a rather grubby handkerchief from his pocket and picks up the glass cautiously. He sniffs inside with extreme care.*

NORRIS Smells all right.

WENDY Yes, I wonder what it... Oh. *(A sudden thought)* That was my glass really, wasn't it?

NORRIS Precisely so.

WENDY *(a little uneasily)* Oh. Me again.

NORRIS *looks at* **BRINTON** *suspiciously.* **BRINTON** *immediately coughs.* **NORRIS** *switches his gaze to* **AMY** *who favours him with one of her grotesque smirks.*

NORRIS Precisely so.

WENDY *(brightening)* What do they say? They always come in threes, don't they?

NORRIS *(grimly)* Let's hope it's just threes.

MORTIMER *returns, followed by* **JOCELYN**.

MORTIMER I'm all right. I'll just go upstairs and get some mouthwash. Rather burnt my mouth, I think.

NORRIS Have you any idea what it was?

JOCELYN Bleach. We think it was bleach.

NORRIS Bleach?

MORTIMER It smells like it. Here. It's all over me where I spilt it. *(He holds out a hand)* Smell.

NORRIS *(sniffing)* Yes. That's bleach.

MORTIMER *(extending the other hand to* **WENDY***)* Bleach?

WENDY *(smelling)* Oh, yes. Parazone, I think.

NORRIS How the hell did that get in a champagne glass?

MORTIMER *(going upstairs)* Don't ask me. Ask the washers-up.

JOCELYN You don't wash glasses in bleach. Not even in this house.

MORTIMER *(as he goes)* I thought you were all supposed to be going out.

MORTIMER *goes off upstairs.*

JOCELYN Heavens, look at the time.

NORRIS Just a minute.

JOCELYN What?

NORRIS We can't go out now.

JOCELYN Why not?

NORRIS Not with...all this.

Under the next, **AMY** *starts to clear away the bowls of nibbles and the glasses on to the tray.*

JOCELYN If you're thinking what I think you're thinking, then under the circumstances it might be the very best thing if we did, don't you think?

WENDY *(to* **AMY***)* Let me help you with these.

AMY It's all right.

WENDY No, please. I'd like to do my share. I can't bear being waited on for too long. It just gives me the fidgets. *(She reaches for* **MORTIMER***'s glass)*

NORRIS *(indicating the glass)* Leave that glass, please.

WENDY Oh, yes.

JOCELYN What are you going to do with it?

NORRIS *(uncertainly)* I'm going to...look at it. At my leisure.

BRINTON Right – I'm... I'm off, anyway. Got a meeting. Arts meeting at seven.

JOCELYN Do you want a lift there, Brinton? We have to go that way in my car.

BRINTON No, no. Cycle. I'll cycle.

JOCELYN It's going to pour with rain in a minute. Are you sure?

BRINTON Yes, yes, I'll cycle. *(He heads towards the study, muttering)* Otherwise I'll have to walk back, won't I?

BRINTON *exits.*

WENDY *(at the doorway to the kitchen)* Through here, is it?

AMY That's right.

WENDY *and* **AMY** *go off to the kitchen.*

JOCELYN Norrie, what are you playing at?

NORRIS *(triumphantly)* It's happened, Joss. It's finally happened.

JOCELYN What has?

NORRIS It's actually happening. To me. In this house within the next few hours, there is every possibility that a murder will be committed.

JOCELYN Oh, Norris.

NORRIS No, Jossy, please, listen. One: the brake nuts on the car loosened deliberately. I saw the marks. Two: the wardrobe in the bedroom unscrewed from the wall, rawlplugs removed and the screws replaced.

JOCELYN It was perfectly secure an hour before she came. We both cleaned the room together, Amy and I.

NORRIS Done subsequently, then. Three: the champagne glass filled with bleach. Three in a row. It's got to be attempted murder, Jossy, it's got to be. And I'm actually here on the spot. Don't you see? Just like it's meant to happen. Like I always dreamt it would happen. *(He looks heavenwards)* Thank you, thank you. I knew I had something coming to me, Jossy, I knew. You can't lead a lousy, miserable, boring life like mine without there being a reward at the end of it somewhere. Present company excepted, Joss. There'd be no point in it all. There'd be no justice. My God, I've earned this. All those endless days of waiting rewarded. *(Heavenward again)* Thank you, thank you. It's amazing, Joss, just amazing. Be happy for me. *(He pauses for breath)*

JOCELYN *(gently)* Norrie.

NORRIS Hm?

JOCELYN Have you followed this through? I mean, if you are right—

NORRIS I am.

JOCELYN Then who are your suspects?

NORRIS *does not reply.*

I'll tell you who they are. There's Brinton. There's Amy. And there's me.

NORRIS Oh, come on.

JOCELYN And you.

NORRIS Me?

JOCELYN Well, we'd all like to see her dead.

NORRIS Ssh.

JOCELYN *(more quietly)* We would. So before you get too carried away, become too convinced there's a possible case for attempted murder, remember it could only be one of us. *(She starts upstairs)* Come on.

NORRIS Where to?

JOCELYN We're going to the cinema.

NORRIS No, I'm sorry, Jossy, not me. I cannot leave here. Not with all this going on. That woman on her own in this house.

JOCELYN She isn't on her own. Mortimer's here. To have his talk with her.

NORRIS I'm sorry, Joss. For the one and only time in my life, I've found myself to be the right man in the right place at the right time.

JOCELYN That's that then. I'll have to go on my own. Mortimer won't like you staying.

NORRIS To hell with him. A woman's life is on the line, isn't it?

JOCELYN Don't get too carried away, will you, Norris?

NORRIS Will you tell Mortimer I'm staying then?

JOCELYN You tell him. I'm not. *(She goes off upstairs)*

NORRIS *again picks up* **MORTIMER***'s glass and holds it up to the light, inspecting it from various angles.*

WENDY *enters from the kitchen and watches* **NORRIS**.

NORRIS *(catching sight of her)* Ah. Just inspecting it for—

WENDY Well, after all you are a detective...

NORRIS I am. Listen, I'm afraid I have to say this. I'm less than happy with the way events have been evolving since you arrived here.

WENDY How do you mean?

NORRIS Well, without in any way wishing to alarm you, I think someone's trying to kill you.

WENDY *(alarmed)* Oh.

NORRIS Keep calm. There have been, to my knowledge, three distinct attempts upon your life in the space of so many hours.

WENDY They couldn't have been accidents?

NORRIS No. Definitely not.

WENDY Oh. Oh, dear. *(She shivers suddenly)* Oh.

NORRIS Don't worry. I intend to stay with you this evening. I'm not going out.

WENDY Thank you. Mr Chalke will be here, of course.

NORRIS I feel you're in need of someone slightly more reliable.

WENDY You.

NORRIS Yes.

WENDY Thank you.

NORRIS I'd suggest you left here now, only it's too late for a train. First thing tomorrow, though.

WENDY Yes.

NORRIS I'll get you home safely. Trust me. *(He winks at her)*

WENDY Of course, it could always be you, couldn't it?

NORRIS What?

WENDY You. Trying to kill me.

NORRIS *laughs at the very thought and shakes his head. He exits upstairs.*

(suddenly very worried) Oh, dear.

Behind her, from the direction of the study, a bicycle comes on, pushed by **BRINTON**, *now in full cycling gear. He rings his bell.*

(jumping) Oh.

BRINTON I like to keep my bike in the billiard room. It's dry in there. Well, it was the billiard room when we had a billiard table. We sold that to the undertaker. After he'd buried Mother. Have a nice evening.

WENDY Thank you.

BRINTON I belong to the local Arts Society. We have meetings every month. Just in the next village. We have a speaker, discussion groups, we look at each other's work. It's all pretty boring. We even had a politician.

WENDY Oh, how interesting.

BRINTON He was especially boring. Beware of politicians that paint.

WENDY Ah. *(She opens the front door for* **BRINTON***)* See you later.

BRINTON I do hope so. Be very, very careful, won't you?

WENDY Yes. Mr Honeywell is going to stay with me.

BRINTON Is he? Ah, bad luck. I'll be back very shortly. Bye.

BRINTON *exits.*

WENDY Goodbye. *(She closes the door)*

JOCELYN *comes down the stairs with her coat on, looking still more apprehensive.*

JOCELYN *(as she descends)* Amy, I'm ready. Amy! She's not going to make me late, is she? *(To* **WENDY***)* Hallo. OK?

WENDY Yes, yes.

JOCELYN I'm just off to the cinema. Don't often get the chance. Did Norris tell you he's staying?

WENDY Oh, yes. I'm very grateful.

JOCELYN I'm sure it's all nothing at all. I'm sure it isn't. Norris does, occasionally...he... Well, he means it for the best.

AMY *comes from the kitchen. She also has her coat on.*

(seeing **AMY***)* And my daughter's off to her...her...drama class, aren't you, Amy?

WENDY Oh. An actress, are you?

AMY No.

JOCELYN I'm giving her a lift.

WENDY What film are you seeing?

JOCELYN It's an oldie called *Double Indemnity*. Do you know it?

WENDY Oh, yes. I've seen it on the television. Three times. Barbara Stanwyck. It's very good indeed.

JOCELYN *(opening the front door)* Yes, I've heard it is. It's one I've always missed. And of course we don't have television. It's the last night. Otherwise I'd—

WENDY Don't be late for it.

JOCELYN No. See you soon. Take care, won't you?

WENDY Yes.

JOCELYN Come on, Amy. *(She opens the front door)*

+++ **BRINTON** *is standing there.*

BRINTON *(accusingly)* Where is my front light? Someone has stolen my front light.

JOCELYN *(reproachfully)* Amy!

AMY *looks round, goes to the side table and retrieves the lamp. She gives it to* **BRINTON**.

AMY *(ungraciously)* Here.

BRINTON Thank you so, so much. You'll be in jail one day. See if you're not.

He goes +++.

JOCELYN *(stepping outside)* Goodness! It is dark out here. You can hardly see your nose. Amy, can I take your hand?

AMY *(to* **WENDY***)* See you later. Possibly.

AMY *exits, closing the front door.*

WENDY *stands alone in the house which seems suddenly very quiet. There is a distant peal of thunder.*

WENDY Oh. *(She hums a little tune to herself and wanders to the piano. She plays a couple of isolated notes, hums and plays two or three more)*

MORTIMER *enters above and stands at the top of the stairs, watching* **WENDY***.*

Unaware, **WENDY** *continues.*

MORTIMER *(applauding her efforts)* Bravo.

WENDY Oh. Hallo.

MORTIMER Haven't lost your touch, I see. *(He comes down the stairs)* Norris tells me he's sacrificed his trip to the cinema in order to sit with you.

WENDY Yes. He's been very kind.

MORTIMER In my opinion whatever peril you may or may not be in, there are few experiences more hazardous than exposing yourself to an evening of undiluted Norris Honeywell. You'll undoubtedly be found dead in your bed. *(He laughs)*

WENDY *(laughing weakly)* Yes.

MORTIMER Perhaps later on we can have our little chat together. Concerning the bequest. I'll just look out all the paperwork. So you can see what you'll be getting.

WENDY Oh, yes. Of course. How exciting.

MORTIMER Supposing you survive that long. *(He laughs and heads for the study)*

WENDY *(unconvincingly laughing with him)* Right.

MORTIMER *stops in the study doorway. He switches off the overhead lights. The room becomes considerably gloomier, lit only by one or two isolated table lamps and by the fire itself.*

MORTIMER You don't mind if I do, do you? We get these whopping electric bills. Oh, by the way, I don't want to scaremonger at all but if someone is intending to do you harm, I'd have thought Honeywell features pretty high on the list of suspects, wouldn't you? Just a thought.

MORTIMER *goes.*

WENDY *makes little noises in her throat.*

NORRIS *appears at the stop of the stairs.*

NORRIS Has everyone gone?

WENDY *(startled)* What? Yes.

NORRIS Right. *(He nearly misses his footing)* Bit dark, isn't it? *(He descends the stairs)* Just us, then.

WENDY Yes. *(She backs away a little)* And Mr Chalke. In there. Within earshot.

NORRIS Oh, yes. Mustn't forget him.

WENDY No.

NORRIS Without in any way being alarmist I think if he or she is planning another attempt on your life, it's going to have to be tonight.

WENDY Yes.

NORRIS That's the way I'd do it.

WENDY Yes.

NORRIS *(sitting)* Well, let 'em come, eh? Let 'em all come. We're ready.

There is distant rumble of thunder.

WENDY *(sitting at a distance from him)* Yes.

They sit on in the firelight waiting.

The lights fade to blackout.

ACT II

Scene One

The same. About forty minutes later.

WENDY *and* **NORRIS** *are in the same chairs; both have dozed off. A distant rumble of thunder.* **NORRIS** *stirs but doesn't wake. In a second,* **MORTIMER** *comes in and regards the scene. He takes out his sheet of paper, consults it briefly, then smiles. He replaces the paper in his pocket and emits a bloodcurdling yell.*

NORRIS *and* **WENDY** *leap in the air.*

NORIS } *(together)* { Eh?
WENDY } { Oh.

MORTIMER I'm so sorry. Did I disturb you?

NORRIS What do you want?

MORTIMER Just wanted to make sure you were both all right.

WENDY Thank you.

NORRIS Perfectly.

MORTIMER I don't think it's a very good idea for both of you to go to asleep at once, is it? Why not take it in turns? Like they do in the Westerns. I'm just getting all the paperwork together, Wendy, for you to have a look at. The will. Various deeds. See what you're getting. I'll bring it all through here where it's warmer. You'll find you own quite a bit of the land round here as well. Plenty of room for dogs.

MORTIMER *exits into his study, barking.*

NORRIS *(watching* **MORTIMER***; muttering)* One of these days, I'm going... *(He checks himself)*

WENDY Sorry?

NORRIS Nothing. He's right, though. We should try and keep awake. Do you play cards, by any chance?

WENDY No, not really.

NORRIS Well, er...what else is there? What about the piano? Do you still play the piano?

WENDY No.

NORRIS Ah, pity. We could have had a concert.

WENDY Yes. I play a little for the children. Well, I did when they were small. But now Gary's fourteen, Graham's eleven and Gilbert's nine, they're a bit old for that sort of thing.

NORRIS What sort of thing's that?

WENDY Well, I used to write them silly songs, you know. I tried to make them a bit instructive as well but they're really only for fun.

NORRIS Go on, then. Give us one of those.

WENDY No, they're silly.

NORRIS Go on.

WENDY *(sitting on the piano stool)* Well, here's a bit of one then. Let's see. *(She plays a chord)* No, sorry. That's not right. Look, I can hardly get my fingers together.

NORRIS *listens to the following with mounting incredulity.*

Singing and playing.

FIVE LITTLE SAUSAGES ALL IN A PAN,
FIZZ, FIZZ, SIZZLE AND FIZZ.
FRYING AWAY JUST AS FAST AS THEY CAN.
FIZZ, FIZZ, SIZZLE AND FIZZ.

SUDDENLY ONE OF THEM JUMPED ON THE FLOOR
FIZZ, FIZZ, SIZZLE AND FIZZ.
ALL THAT ARE LEFT IN THE PAN ARE JUST—

(speaking) Then you're supposed to say "four". All right?

NORRIS *nods.*

WENDY *(repeating the last line, singing)*
ALL THAT ARE LEFT IN THE PAN ARE JUST—

NORRIS
WENDY } *(together)* Four.

WENDY *(speaking)* That's it.

Singing.

FIZZ, FIZZ, SIZZLE AND FIZZ.
FOUR LITTLE SAUSAGES ALL IN A PAN
FIZZ, FIZZ, SIZZLE AND FIZZ.

There is an enormous clap of thunder.

Her voice going up a register; singing.

FRYING AWAY JUST AS FAST AS THEY CAN.
FIZZ, FIZZ, SIZZLE AND FIZZ.
DADDY CAME HOME AND HAD ONE FOR HIS TEA.
FIZZ, FIZZ, SIZZLE AND FIZZ.
ALL THAT ARE LEFT IN THE PAN ARE JUST—

A loud clatter from the kitchen. **WENDY** *stops playing.*

(in a whisper) What was that?

NORRIS From the kitchen.

WENDY Someone's out there.

NORRIS Could be the wind. Or Mortimer.

WENDY He's in his study. Isn't he?

NORRIS There's a way through. Via the dining-room. *(Calling towards the study)* Mortimer! Hey, Mortimer.

MORTIMER *(offstage; distantly, from the study)* Hallo. Somebody call?

NORRIS Was that you in the kitchen just then?

MORTIMER *(offstage; distant)* No.

NORRIS Are you sure?

MORTIMER *(offstage)* I've been in here. I'm busy. Go away.

NORRIS *deliberates.*

NORRIS Wait here. I won't be one second.

WENDY Don't leave me for too long.

NORRIS You see anything at all, you shout.

WENDY Yes.

NORRIS *goes off cautiously to the kitchen.*

Singing under her breath.

FIZZ, FIZZ, SIZZLE AND FIZZ.
THREE LITTLE SAUSAGES ALL IN THE PAN
FIZZ, FIZZ, SIZZLE AND FIZZ.

The handle of the front door turns. **WENDY***'s eyes are slowly drawn to the front door.*

FRYING AWAY JUST AS – FAST – AS THEY CAN...

The handle becomes more agitated. The door begins to shake.

FIZZ, FIZZ, SIZZLE AND—

(in a low voice; speaking) Mr Honeywell.

The handle suddenly rattles with tremendous vigour, and the door is shaken as though something huge is trying to enter.

(screaming) Mr Honeywell! Quickly, Mr Honeywell!

NORRIS *comes racing back in from the kitchen.*

NORRIS Where? Where? What? What?

WENDY The door. Someone's trying to get in.

NORRIS *wrestles with the door and flings it open. There is no-one there. He looks out cautiously. There is a flash of lightning.*

Be careful.

NORRIS Nobody. Sure you weren't imagining it?

WENDY The handle was moving. I saw it.

NORRIS Right. I believe you. *(He closes the door and bolts it)* That should stop them. By the way, you'd better call me Norris. It's quicker to shout than Mr Honeywell.

WENDY Right. Norris.

There is a clap of thunder.

Oh, dear.

Distantly, the dinner gong sounds insistently and violently.

(hysterically) What now?

NORRIS Someone's playing a little game, that's all.

WENDY Do you think it's possible we could go and stay in a hotel, do you think?

NORRIS It's possible. We don't have a car. Apart from one with dodgy brakes. And I don't fancy walking three miles in the dark, do you? But it's possible.

WENDY No.

MORTIMER *enters from the study.*

MORTIMER Was that you?

NORRIS What?

MORTIMER Banging that infernal gong.

NORRIS No, it wasn't.

MORTIMER Well, who else could it have been?

NORRIS That's what I'd like to know.

MORTIMER If you'd feel any safer with me than him, you're welcome to sit in my study, Wendy—

WENDY I'll be all right, thank you.

MORTIMER Was that you playing the piano?

WENDY Yes.

MORTIMER Yes. I remember you as having very little talent indeed. I think I over-estimated you.

MORTIMER *exits.*

NORRIS I prefer your music to his.

WENDY Thank you.

NORRIS Mind you, I'm completely tone deaf so don't get too encouraged.

NORRIS *goes to the window.*

WENDY Do you see anything?

NORRIS No. It's pitch dark, I can't see—

There is more lightning, followed almost immediately by thunder.

What the—?

WENDY What is it?

NORRIS I saw someone then. I thought I did. In the middle of the lawn. Just when the lightning... There's somebody out there all right.

WENDY *makes a moaning sound.*

Now, don't be nervous. We stick together, all right?

WENDY Yes.

The lights suddenly dip so that the lamps now merely glimmer and the room is lit predominantly by firelight, giving it an eerie feeling.

What's happening?

NORRIS Just a power reduction. Must be the storm. We must just pray they don't go altogether. I don't fancy creeping round this place in the dark.

More lightning and thunder.

(uneasily) You wouldn't like to play us another tune, would you? Keep the morale up?

WENDY Yes. What should I—?

NORRIS I don't mind. I'm not fussy. Another verse of the old sausage saga wouldn't go amiss.

WENDY Yes, I'll... *(She sits at the piano and forces herself to play, though her voice and fingers are far from steady)*

NORRIS *stands, casting continual glances around him as if expecting a sudden attack on all sides.*

Singing.

ONE LITTLE SAUSAGE ALONE IN THE PAN
FIZZ, FIZZ, SIZZLE AND FIZZ.
FRYING AWAY JUST AS FAST AS HE CAN.
FIZZ, FIZZ, SIZZLE AND FIZZ.
GARY HAS EATEN HIM 'COS HE WAS DONE
FIZZ, FIZZ, SIZZLE AND FIZ.
ALL THAT IS LEFT IN THE PAN NOW IS...

NORRIS
WENDY } *(together)* None.

WENDY *(singing)*
FIZZ, FIZZ, SIZZLE AND—

She is interrupted, this time by a loud crash from upstairs as if the wardrobe has again fallen.

(shrilly) There's somebody upstairs now.

NORRIS Ssh. *(He takes the poker from the fireplace; very quietly to* **WENDY***)* Don't make a sound.

WENDY *(mouthing)* Don't leave me.

NORRIS Ssh. *(He reaches the bottom of the stairs)*

Something circular, and looking at first glance unpleasantly like a human head, rolls down the stairs.

WENDY *screams,* **NORRIS** *screams almost as loudly. He leaps up and down and beats thin air with the poker.* **WENDY** *clambers up on the piano stool. They both calm down.*

NORRIS *investigates the grisly object. It turns out, on closer investigation, to be no more than a doll's head, large and quite lifelike.*

WENDY What is it?

NORRIS It's a doll's head. One of Amy's old dolls. Been torn off. I think it's about time we sorted this joker out.

WENDY How?

NORRIS I'm going upstairs to find out who it is.

WENDY Aren't you afraid?

NORRIS Yes, frankly. Bloody terrified. But I'm going to get even more frightened sitting here.

WENDY Can I come with you?

NORRIS You'd better not.

WENDY But I'll be on my own.

There is the sound of a door slamming upstairs.

NORRIS Do you hear that? They're up there. You're down here. Now, I'll tell you what we'll do. You sit down at that piano and you start singing as loud as you can. So wherever I am upstairs, I'll be able to hear you. If they do manage to slip past me, the second you stop singing, I'll be down here fourteen seconds later, all right?

WENDY Yes.

NORRIS Good girl.

WENDY Yes.

NORRIS *(trying to make light of it)* And if you hear me start singing, that means I need you upstairs in fourteen seconds, all right?

WENDY *(smiling feebly)* Yes.

NORRIS Come on then. Off you go.

WENDY *sits at the piano again. Her teeth are chattering and she is obviously terrified. She opens and shuts her mouth but only little squeaks come out.*

WENDY *(trying again, singing feebly)*
THIS IS THE SONG OF A—

(she breaks off, apologetically) Sorry.

NORRIS Come on, you can do it.

WENDY *(starting again to sing with the piano; during the following this song recital becomes more frenetic)*
THIS IS THE SONG OF A PERSON CALLED PETER
WHO LIVES THERE INSIDE EVERY NIGHT STORAGE HEATER.
WE SWITCH OFF THE LIGHTS IN THE NIGHT SO HE'LL SPY
IT'S TIME THAT HE TURNED ALL THE HEATING UP HIGH.

She stops, then starts another song.

HALLO, MERRY LITTLE GOBLIN,

I'M SURE I SAW YOU FIRST,
A-SPLASHING IN OUR KETTLE
AND WHISTLING FIT TO BURST.

NORRIS *climbs the stairs and disappears.*

Singing.

HEY HO, IT'S JELLY FOR TEA!
GUESS WHO'S HAVING SOME, WHO CAN IT BE?
GARY AND GRAHAM AND GILBERT AND ME.
TEE-HEE-HEE-TEE-HEE-HEE-TEE-HEE-HEE-HEE.

Starting another song.

UP POPS THE TASTY TOASTIE
DARK BROWN AND NICELY ROASTIE
THE WAY I LIKE IT MOSTY
I LOVE MY TASTY TOASTIE.

Her repertoire is beginning to run low.

TWELVE LITTLE SAUSAGES ALL IN A PAN—

As she starts to sing this, **MORTIMER** *enters from the study. He walks stiffly with eyes glazed.*

MORTIMER *moves towards* **WENDY,** *one arm outstretched; in his other hand he clutches his award. In the firelight, we see blood is running down* **MORTIMER***'s face from a wound in his head.*

Trilling away, unaware.

FIZZ, FIZZ, SIZZLE AND FIZZ.
FRYING AWAY JUST AS FAST AS THEY CAN.
FIZZ, FIZZ, SIZZLE AND FIZZ.
ONE OF THEM—

MORTIMER*'s hand touches* **WENDY***'s shoulder. The words freeze in* **WENDY***'s throat. She stops singing and playing. Despite herself, she is forced to turn round to see who's behind her.*

MORTIMER *(as she faces him; in a hoarse whisper)* Help me... Please help me... *(He collapses in a heap at* **WENDY***'s feet, releasing his award)*

WENDY *stares in horror. From the study, suddenly, there comes the sound of shattering glass like a window breaking. This is the final straw for* **WENDY** *and she lets out a mighty scream.*

NORRIS *enters above and comes racing down the stairs, not at first seeing* **MORTIMER***'s body.*

NORRIS Wendy? Wendy?

WENDY *stands, pointing at* **MORTIMER***, unable to speak.*

Oh, my God. *(He kneels by* **MORTIMER** *to examine him. He withdraws his hand and rises staring at it)* Blood...it's blood...

WENDY *opens her mouth to scream again.*

Please. No. Don't do that again, please. *(He kneels again beside* **MORTIMER***. After a moment)* He's dead.

WENDY *stifles a scream. There is a slow, measured, heavy knocking on the door as of something non-human.*

WENDY What's that?

NORRIS I don't know. *(More calmly)* I don't know. Just a second, I'll see.

The banging comes again. **NORRIS** *unbolts and opens the door cautiously.*

A bicycle wheel is pushed into view, followed by **BRINTON***.*

BRINTON Hallo.

NORRIS What are you doing back here?

BRINTON The chain broke on my bike. Look. See? I cycled half-way there and this happens. I had to walk back in the pouring— *(He stops as he sees* **MORTIMER***)* What's happened to him?

NORRIS *(grimly)* I'm sorry to tell you there's been a fatal accident.

BRINTON Oh. *(He stares at* **MORTIMER***)* Is he dead?

NORRIS Yes.

BRINTON *(it's difficult to tell if he's disappointed or not)* Ah.

NORRIS Looks like we've got a full blown murder now.

A low rumble of thunder.

I'll go and phone. *(He makes to move towards the study)*

WENDY Be careful!

NORRIS What?

WENDY I heard someone in there.

NORRIS When?

WENDY Just now. Breaking a window, it sounded like.

NORRIS *(to* **WENDY***)* You stay there. *(To* **BRINTON***)* You come with me.

BRINTON Me?

NORRIS Come on. They may still be in there.

BRINTON Why can't I stay here?

NORRIS Come on!

BRINTON *(protesting)* They may still be in there.

NORRIS Shh! *(To* **WENDY***)* Back in a tick.

WENDY Yes.

NORRIS *and* **BRINTON** *go off cautiously towards the study, the latter still pushing his bike.*

WENDY *waits apprehensively. She looks down nervously at* **MORTIMER**. *She sees the award which he dropped as he fell. Gingerly she picks it up and examines it. She looks towards the study, a trifle puzzled now. As she hears someone coming she hastily puts the award on the piano.*

NORRIS *sticks his head round the door.*

NORRIS Clean away. Whoever it was. Broke in through the french window, it looks like.

WENDY Oh.

NORRIS I'd better phone the police, I suppose. *(He reflects)* That's a pity.

As he goes back to the study, **WENDY** *again picks up the award.*

WENDY *(softly)* Oh, dear. It could be any one of them.

The lights fade to blackout.

Scene Two

The same. The next day, mid-Sunday morning. We see the house in daylight for the first time. It is a cold, sunny morning.

On the table near the front door, which is ajar, is a uniform police inspector's hat. On the piano is **MORTIMER***'s award, pristine. The cycle lamp, if it hasn't already done so, has gone. The main table is covered with breakfast things. It is apparent from this that some people have eaten while others haven't. Of the five places laid, two are finished with. One (***WENDY***'s) is untouched whilst at the fourth,* **JOCELYN** *sits eating a piece of toast rather abstractedly. At the fifth place there is a half-eaten piece of toast as if the occupant had momentarily left the room.*

This, it transpires, is **NORRIS***, who now strides in from the garden. He is full of the thrill of the chase, and, as never before, has become a man with a purpose.*

JOCELYN Norrie, do finish your breakfast.

NORRIS *(in his own world)* What?

JOCELYN Your breakfast.

NORRIS Yes, yes. *(He picks up his piece of toast)* It's exactly like your books, Joss. Word for word. You don't realize how accurate you are, girl. I'm amazed they haven't caught on. You got it all dead right. Right down to the stupid policeman. Running round in circles asking the wrong questions to the wrong people. Accidentally standing on the evidence. I even had him saying to me, "We can manage without your help, thank you very much, sir." Now he's lost his hat, the stupid git.

JOCELYN *(indicating)* There.

NORRIS Ah.

JOCELYN Have they come to any conclusions? As to who they think did it?

NORRIS *(scornfully)* Intruders. That's their theory. Two of them, they've decided. Maybe more. Perhaps a gang. Possibly a coach party. One got in the upstairs window via the ladder. That's the one I heard. Another broke in through the windows in the study and clobbered Mortimer.

JOCELYN Well, it's possible.

NORRIS Oh yes, very possible. Probably part of a government young burglars' training scheme. Blokes upstairs on ladders. Fellows breaking in through windows. One rattling the front door handle. And three more falling over the dinner gong. Bloody load of nonsense. I gave them that wine glass. I said to the sergeant, "Never mind the window, you fingerprint this, matey." Do you know what he said to me? "Certainly, if you'll put a little something in it first." Sarcastic berk. All right then, so be it. I shall have to carry on this murder enquiry on my own, won't I? See you in a minute.

JOCELYN Norrie.

NORRIS *turns back.*

Don't...get under their feet, will you?

NORRIS Their feet? That would be hard to avoid. They can't even find the murder weapon. What about that?

JOCELYN Really? Well maybe...maybe they took it with them?

NORRIS Who took it with them?

JOCELYN The intruders.

NORRIS *(scornfully)* Wild geese, Joss, wild geese!

JOCELYN Do you have a better solution, then?

NORRIS *(without total conviction)* Oh, yes. Pieces of the jigsaw are slotting into place.

JOCELYN Crossing off the suspects?

NORRIS Yes.

JOCELYN Am I still on the list?

NORRIS Certainly not. You were at the cinema.

JOCELYN Yes.

NORRIS With Amy.

JOCELYN Yes.

NORRIS She just told me. She said she decided at the last minute to skip her drama class and come with you to the film. That's correct?

JOCELYN *(only the slightest hesitation)* Oh, yes.

NORRIS So that rules you both out. Joint alibi. And Brinton, we know, cycled three miles for his meeting till his chain broke and then walked three miles back. Which puts him in the clear.

JOCELYN Then we're back to intruders, aren't we?

NORRIS I'm working on another angle altogether.

JOCELYN Do be careful, Norrie.

NORRIS Why?

JOCELYN About whom you accuse. I don't want you to get the wrong person by mistake.

NORRIS *(coolly)* That's not worthy of you, Jossy, that remark.

JOCELYN I'm sorry.

NORRIS Don't lose faith. Not now. Keep the faith. *(He goes to the front door)*

BRINTON *enters through the front door, nearly colliding with* **NORRIS**.

BRINTON Are they going now, those policemen?

NORRIS Don't ask me.

NORRIS *picks up the policeman's hat and exits through the front door with it.*

BRINTON They've been staring at me through my studio window. Pulling faces.

JOCELYN I don't think they'd be doing that, Brinton. Not the police force.

BRINTON He did. I was just...looking out to see what they were doing and this detective went— *(He demonstrates by waggling his fingers by his ears, sticking his tongue out and pulling a face)* He did. Honestly.

AMY *enters from the kitchen with a tray.*

I'm just going to get my scarf. It's very cold out there.

BRINTON *exits to the kitchen.*

AMY *starts to clear the table.*

JOCELYN *(to* **AMY***)* What are you doing?

AMY Clearing away.

JOCELYN Well, don't clear it all. Wendy hasn't had anything yet.

AMY Oh. Having a lie-in, is she?

JOCELYN Amy, don't. She's had a terrible shock. She's going this morning.

AMY Hooray.

JOCELYN Did you... Did you tell the police as well that you went to the cinema with me?

AMY *looks out of the window.*

It's a good job one of them mentioned it. I was able to back you up. Been a fine thing if we'd both had different stories.

There is a pause.

Why? Why tell them that?

AMY *(expressionless)* Why do you think?

JOCELYN They think it's an intruder.

AMY *laughs mirthlessly and goes back towards the kitchen.*

BRINTON *enters from the kitchen and almost collides with* **AMY** *in the doorway.*

BRINTON *(ignoring* **AMY***; to* **JOCELYN***)* Is Wendy coming down?

AMY *exits.*

JOCELYN I hope so. She's catching a train.

BRINTON Ah.

JOCELYN Why?

BRINTON Nothing. *(He turns at the front door with a sudden thought)* I say, nothing could have happened to her, do you think? In the night?

JOCELYN *looks blank.*

No. Silly.

BRINTON *goes out of the front door.*

JOCELYN *(after a second)* Oh, dear God. *(She jumps up and calls)* Wendy! Wendy! *(She runs to the stairs)*

WENDY *appears at the top of the stairs. She carries both her cases, the large one and the small vanity case, plus her coat. She heads down the stairs during the following.*

WENDY Morning.

JOCELYN Oh. Good.

WENDY Anything wrong?

JOCELYN No. I just had an awful thought you'd...overslept.

WENDY Oh, no.

JOCELYN We were all very late. Time the police had finished.

WENDY They're back this morning I see. Beating the bushes. Hive of industry.

JOCELYN Yes. *(Offering to help* **WENDY***)* Here, let me...

WENDY *has reached the bottom of the stairs.* **JOCELYN** *takes the larger case from her and puts it near the door.*

WENDY Thank you.

JOCELYN Would you care for some breakfast?

WENDY Just a little toast. And some cereal. That'll do me fine.

JOCELYN Sure? *(She indicates a chair)* Sit here. I'll get you some more toast. This is inedible. *(Calling)* Amy. Amy. Make some more toast, would you, please? *(She pauses to listen)* Amy?

AMY *(offstage, from the kitchen)* All right.

JOCELYN *(calling)* And make some more... *(To* **WENDY***)* Coffee?

WENDY Tea, please, if that's at all convenient.

JOCELYN *(calling)* Make some tea. *(To* **WENDY***)* She won't be a minute. I thought you could try for the one-o-five. It's a slowish train but it's about the best they can offer on a Sunday. I've booked a taxi. I'd have run you there myself only the police don't want us leaving the house. I suppose that means we're all still under suspicion. Intruders or no.

WENDY I suppose so. They said they'd finished with me. I mustn't leave the country, that's all. I said what with fourteen budgies, two parrots, eight hamsters, six white rats and an expectant Labrador? I'd be so lucky.

JOCELYN I rang your husband back and he's going to meet you at the other end. He was obviously very concerned.

WENDY Oh, yes. Yes, he would be.

JOCELYN I told him you were fine.

WENDY Yes. He'll be upset. Probably get a bit cross with me.

JOCELYN Cross?

WENDY Yes, Ollie usually does if I get into trouble. He sort of stands and shouts and bangs things. Funny. He's always been like that. I was knocked down by a car a couple of years ago, not seriously but – you know – we were both out shopping and there I was, lying in the road, outside Woolworth's and he just stood there shouting at me. "You stupid, so-and-so woman" – you know. Great big crowd round us. I think it's just his way of saying he loves me.

JOCELYN Yes.

WENDY I don't know what he'd do if he found out someone had been trying to kill me. Probably murder me.

JOCELYN Yes. *(She indicates the cereal packets)* Would you like any of these while you're waiting?

WENDY Oh, yes. Why not? *(She selects a packet)* I'll have some of these. They're Gilbert's favourites.

JOCELYN Ah.

WENDY Only he has them with treacle.

JOCELYN Milk? Sugar?

WENDY Thank you very much.

JOCELYN You don't want any treacle?

WENDY *(helping herself)* Oh, no. *(She catches sight of something through the window)* Who's that sitting out there...? Oh, it's...er...isn't it?

JOCELYN *(looking)* Brinton.

WENDY Yes. He a very nice man, isn't he? Gentle. For a man.

JOCELYN Yes. Mostly.

Pause.

Did you... Did you see anything at all last night? That would have led you to suspect who it was?

WENDY Not really, no, I didn't.

JOCELYN The police are not ruling out an intruder. But—

WENDY No, I don't think it was an intruder.

JOCELYN *(seeming relieved)* Be very convenient though, wouldn't it? So you're none the wiser either?

WENDY Well, I do have a little theory...

JOCELYN You do?

WENDY Yes. Not about who...killed Mr Chalke. I really don't know about that. But I was lying there this morning before I got up and I think I can see, perhaps, how the other things might have happened. And why they happened. The things that happened or nearly happened to me. If you see what I mean.

JOCELYN And?

WENDY I think Mortimer arranged it all, you know. Does that sound strange?

JOCELYN No. Look. I was going to show you.

During the following, **JOCELYN** *goes to her book on the table, opens it and produces a folded typewritten page hidden between the leaves.*

Last night when I got back to all the commotion, I found this. It's typewritten but it has to be Mortimer's. He must have dropped it. I'm afraid I picked it up and kept it. It's a list. Some sort of master list. Everything. Look see? "Brakes." That's the brakes failing on the car – I think he fixed them after you'd arrived here.

WENDY Oh yes, that crossed my mind. When he was pretending to check them, he was really loosening them.

JOCELYN He never lost control. And before that, even, there was Annie, you know the old lady he says he popped in to visit on the way back... *(She shows* **WENDY** *the page)* Look: "magazines". What if he just pretended to visit her?

WENDY But instead he ran up the back lane, climbed the ladder and fixed the wardrobe.

JOCELYN *(showing* **WENDY** *the page)* "Screws". Or finished the job off, anyway. Which explains why the ladder was so handy. *(She shows* **WENDY** *the page again)* "Ladder".

WENDY But he didn't have time to put it away afterwards, of course.

JOCELYN And the champagne—

WENDY Never happened, did it?

JOCELYN He had the bleach ready so he could splash a bit on his hands when he rushed into the kitchen. *(She shows* **WENDY** *the page)* "Bleach".

WENDY Explains the smell.

JOCELYN Never anything in the glass at all.

WENDY No, I thought there couldn't have been. I mean, look at your rug. If he'd spilt bleach on it, you'd know about it by now.

JOCELYN There we are then.

WENDY Aren't we clever?

JOCELYN There's...no mention of a will here.

WENDY I don't think he made one, you know.

JOCELYN No. I have to confess I had a quick look this morning but... Unless it's with the solicitors...

WENDY I don't think he ever had any intention of...leaving all this to me. I think he just wanted to hurt people.

JOCELYN He was a very cruel man sometimes.

WENDY Disappointed. *(She indicates the list)* Should you show that to the police?

JOCELYN I don't know. After all, it doesn't have any real bearing on the murder, does it?

WENDY Probably not.

There is a slight pause.

JOCELYN I suppose we have Mother to blame, bless her. She was a deeply artistic woman, you know... No talent herself but with this great frustrated love of the arts with a capital A. And as so often happens, she married the worst possible man for her, God knows why. They never got on. She was really very beautiful. She could have—

WENDY Yes, she was a lovely woman. Elegant.

JOCELYN Of course, you met her, didn't you?

WENDY Very briefly. She once gave me some lemonade. Home-made.

JOCELYN Father made a great deal of money and caused an equivalent amount of misery while doing so. I don't think Mother with all her ideals and liberal inclinations ever quite forgave herself for being a part of him for as long as she was. Because she was, despite everything, very loyal. But I think her secret plan always was to raise her three offspring as children of light, as it were. All of us painting, sculpting, writing and composing as if somehow we could restore the imbalance created by Father. She felt the arts really were the true weapon to use against evil and we were to be her little shining knights, setting out on our respective steeds – Music, Literature, Painting – righting all wrongs. Unfortunately none of us, it later turned out, was able to ride... *** Oh! *(For the first time, she catches sight of* **MORTIMER***'s award on the piano)*

WENDY *watches* **JOCELYN**.

JOCELYN *turns away sharply, aware of* **WENDY***'s attention.*

WENDY Sorry?

JOCELYN Nothing. I was just... Anyway, *** I think Brinton and I – we accepted that fairly early on. Just went through the artistic motions... Whereas Mortimer... Mortimer wasn't ever going to admit that he was no good as a composer. He never gave up. And when he'd gone thirty years with not a single commission or a solitary acceptance, well...if you can't blame yourself – you blame everyone else, don't you? Publishers, the media, other composers. God, he simply loathed Michael Tippett... And of course he blamed us, his family, too. But I'm afraid, over the years, more and more, the enemy became Norris. Norris who never bought a painting. Never hummed a tune because he couldn't recognize one. Norris who never even read a book. Well, not one that mattered.

WENDY Was it all to get back at Norris?

JOCELYN I think so. Mostly. And to frighten us. Make Norris look a fool. Humiliate him. He nearly succeeded. I'm afraid you just got caught in the middle.

WENDY Story of my life really. *(She laughs)* It still doesn't explain who killed him, though, does it?

JOCELYN Look, I am sorry. It's my family and I'm very sorry that you've become involved in all this. If there's anything we can do. Anything. I'm afraid we don't have any money but—

WENDY You can send me my train fare, if you like.

JOCELYN My pleasure.

AMY *comes in with a pot of tea.*

(replacing the sheet of paper in her book) Where have you been?

AMY Making it.

JOCELYN You took your time, didn't you? Where's the toast, then? Wendy wants some toast.

AMY It's coming.

JOCELYN *smiles apologetically to* **WENDY**.

AMY *goes out to the kitchen.*

JOCELYN *(pouring* **WENDY** *some tea)* Here you are, you must be dying for this.

WENDY Thank you.

JOCELYN Milk?

WENDY Please.

JOCELYN *(pouring very pale tea)* Oh, look at this. She is hopeless really.

WENDY No, that's perfect, perfect. I don't like it too strong.

JOCELYN *(rising)* I must just see if the police want anything. Make sure Norris isn't...annoying them... *(Awkwardly)* Er... it's an awful thing to ask you but Norris is... Well, he's trying to solve this business himself. You may have noticed.

WENDY Yes, I had noticed.

JOCELYN Now, he's... Norris is the nicest, kindest man I've ever known and I'd have absolutely fallen to pieces without him. He tells me every single morning I'm a genius and there are some days I nearly believe him. Now. Almost certainly, he's going to solve the crime, or at any rate he'll come up with a solution. And almost equally certainly – this is a dreadful thing to say, you're going to think me dreadfully disloyal – he's going to get it wrong. Isn't that an awful thing for me to say? But I do know him. Simply, if he does solve it, and if no-one's likely to get hurt as a result, could you possibly humour him? He's a stupid, silly man sometimes but I do love him most frightfully and I'd do anything not to see him hurt.

WENDY I'll do my best. He sounds a bit like Ollie.

AMY *returns with the toast.*

JOCELYN Thank you. *(She sees* **AMY***)* Here we are. Toast at last. See you in a minute.

WENDY How was the film, by the way?

JOCELYN The film? Oh, the film. Marvellous. Wasn't it, Amy?

AMY What?

JOCELYN The film? Wasn't it good?

AMY *(without expression)* Brilliant.

JOCELYN *(to* **WENDY***)* You were quite right.

WENDY Wasn't she wonderful?

JOCELYN Oh, she's a joy. *** And then James Cagney, he always gets me. I only have to see him, I go weak at the knees for some reason. *** Back in a minute. *(In a low voice)* Amy, now stay and talk to our guest.

AMY Me?

JOCELYN Yes, you. Entertain Wendy.

WENDY Oh, there's no need.

JOCELYN Yes, there is. Do her good.

JOCELYN *exits towards the study.*

WENDY *smiles rather embarrassedly at* **AMY**. **AMY** *sits at the other end of the table, and starts to eat cereal from the packet. She makes no effort to communicate. There is an awkward silence.*

WENDY *(unable to bear it any longer)* Sunnier today. After the rain.

There is a pause.

Brinton out there, sitting on the lawn. Didn't know it was warm enough for that. *(She smiles)*

AMY *crunches but does not respond.*

NORRIS *enters through the front door, unlocking it before him and closing it behind him.*

Excuse me, I think Mrs – Jocelyn's looking for... *(She tails off)*

NORRIS, *ignoring* **WENDY** *and* **AMY** *completely, marches across the room and goes off upstairs, deep in thought. The women watch him.* **WENDY** *attempts to eat but has a little difficulty swallowing. She searches for a table napkin but finds she hasn't been given one.*

AMY *(watching* **WENDY**; *amused)* I'm afraid we don't run to table linen.

WENDY Oh, never mind.

AMY Can't get the laundresses like we used to.

WENDY Ah. *(She picks up her vanity case, puts it on the chair beside her, opens it and finds a tissue)*

AMY And paper ones are so frightfully common, don't you agree?

WENDY Handy.

AMY Handy but common.

A pause.

WENDY You don't have to stay with me if you've got things to do. I'm sure you have.

AMY No, no. I've been instructed to entertain you.

WENDY Well, I can make my own amusements, you know.

AMY I'm afraid I'm the untalented one in the family. Everybody else does something. Or pretends to do something. Me, I'm a complete disappointment. All I can do is eat, actually. Not very entertaining. Still, I'll have a try. After all, I've been to dancing classes and singing lessons and piano lessons and art classes and pottery sessions. I've even done a summer school in mime at a disused monastery near Selby so I should be able to do something. *(She rises)*

WENDY *(feebly)* You really don't have to.

AMY *(moving to the piano)* Got to keep my end up, haven't I! *(She sits on the piano stool and plays an horrendous series of discords by way of accompaniment to her singing, which is appalling)*
OH, I DO LIKE TO BE BESIDE THE SEA-SIDE.
OH, I DO LIKE TO BE BESIDE THE SEA.

(she stops; speaking) Sorry, I don't know any more.

WENDY *(smiling weakly)* Thank heavens for that.

AMY Right. Next. *(She springs up)* A bit of dance. *(She does an appalling dance number, lasting all of ten seconds)* There. Too out of condition for that. OK? You don't look very happy.

WENDY I just wonder why you're bothering.

AMY Sorry?

WENDY I mean, I'm not really very important. I'm going in a minute. Why are you bothering to do all this?

AMY Because you're a guest. An honoured guest.

WENDY I see.

> **AMY** *sits next to* **WENDY** *at the table. She picks up* **WENDY***'s vanity case and, placing it on the table in front of her, opens it and begins to go through it.* ••• *As she does so, she hums to herself a brief but clearly recognizable snatch of* **WENDY***'s sausage song* •••

AMY *(exploring the case)* Oh ho! What have we here?

WENDY *(tensely)* Don't do that, please.

AMY No?

WENDY No. Those are private and...personal items in there.

AMY Oh, yes. So they are. *(She pushes the still-opened case to the centre of the table)* Have you had enough breakfast?

WENDY Yes, thank you.

AMY You might get hungry on the train, though. Perhaps you'd like to take something for your journey.

WENDY No, it's quite all right.

AMY Look, marmalade. Here, take some marmalade. *(She puts the jar of marmalade into* **WENDY**'s *case)*

WENDY Now, don't do that. That's silly.

AMY No, you'll be hungry. What else? Butter. There we go. *(She drops the butter dish into the case)*

WENDY *(sitting very bolt upright)* Will you stop that, now?

AMY *(picking up a packet of cereal)* What are these, then? Cornflakes. OK. Fancy some cornflakes? *(She scatters the packet liberally into* **WENDY**'s *case)* And sugar. Must have sugar. *(She empties the sugar bowl into the case)* And milk. Of course, milk. There we are. Can't forget milk. *(She empties the milk jug into the case)*

WENDY *watches* **AMY**. **AMY** *slams the case shut, locks it, shakes it up and replaces it beside* **WENDY**.

All ready for the journey. OK? *(She stands at the other end of the table, smiling at* **WENDY**)

WENDY *regards* **AMY** *for a second.*

WENDY That made you feel better, has it?

AMY, *still smiling, sits at the end of the table.*

I hope so. Because I've never seen such disgraceful behaviour in all my life.

Silence. **AMY** *begins to cry; awful, heavy, heaving sobs.*

(seeming unimpressed) I don't know what you're crying for. It's me who should be crying. Look at my case, you daft little bugger.

AMY *sobs.*

Now what am I going to do with it? *(Pause)* By the time I get home, I'll have a suitcase full of cheese. *(A slight pause)* Have you done?

AMY *subsides a little.*

Daft little bugger.

AMY *(in a tiny little voice)* I'm sorry.

WENDY *(opening her case gingerly an inch or so)* Oh, dear heaven, look at it. *(She closes the lid and looks at* **AMY**. *Despite herself, she laughs)*

AMY *stares at* **WENDY**, *surprised.* **WENDY** *laughs again. Finally,* **AMY** *joins her.*

(subsiding) You should be locked up, you should.

AMY *(likewise)* I know.

WENDY Glad there wasn't any treacle.

AMY I'm sorry. I'll clean it up for you. I'll replace what I can with mine.

WENDY Pardon my asking, but do you do a lot of that sort of thing?

AMY When I'm miserable.

WENDY No wonder you're miserable. Perhaps you should go out a bit more.

AMY Where?

WENDY Well, it sometimes helps to get away.

AMY I can't leave here.

WENDY Why not?

AMY I can't.

WENDY Frightened, are you?

AMY No.

WENDY We could maybe find you a little job. Just temporary.

AMY *(scornfully)* What, in the pet shop, you mean? Cleaning out the parrots?

WENDY Certainly not. I wouldn't let you near my animals. You can work in the paper shop. Think about it. You'd have to move away.

AMY Yes.

WENDY Start very early. Six o'clock.

AMY I'm not qualified.

WENDY Can you read numbers?

AMY Yes.

WENDY Ride a bike?

AMY Yes.

WENDY Then you're qualified.

AMY ••• Oh.

At this point, for the first time, she catches sight of **MORTIMER***'s award on the piano.*

WENDY *watches* **AMY***.*

AMY *turns away sharply, aware that* **WENDY** *is watching her.*

WENDY Sorry?

AMY Nothing. I was just... ••• *(She picks up the case and goes towards the kitchen)* I'll bring this back.

AMY *exits.*

WENDY You better had. Gilbert gave me that. Ten weeks' pocket money that cost him. *(She stands. She is thoughtful)*

There is a knocking on the front door. **WENDY** *hesitates, then decides to open the door.*

BRINTON *stands in the doorway. He holds one hand inside his overcoat.*

BRINTON Ah. I...er... I've been wanting to speak to you. *(He coughs)*

WENDY Yes?

JOCELYN *returns from the direction of the study rather hurriedly.*

JOCELYN Who on earth is—? *(She sees* **BRINTON***)* Oh, I might have guessed.

BRINTON *(rather aggressively)* Yes.

JOCELYN What are you doing?

BRINTON Why?

JOCELYN Why are you standing like that? You look like Napoleon.

BRINTON Napoleon who?

JOCELYN Oh, God. *(She moves to the table as if about to clear it)*

NORRIS *appears on the stairs.*

NORRIS *(confidentially)* Er—

JOCELYN Hallo.

NORRIS Could I have a word, Joss?

JOCELYN All right. *(To* **WENDY***)* Excuse me. *(She joins* **NORRIS** *on the stairs)*

BRINTON *stands like a man waiting for the right moment.* **WENDY** *picks up her large case, places it on a chair and unpacks a cardigan which she puts on during the next.*

NORRIS *(confidentially)* I wonder if you'd mind assembling everyone in this room in about five minutes.

JOCELYN Everyone?

NORRIS I've one or two bombshells to drop.

JOCELYN Are you sure?

NORRIS I am positive, Joss.

JOCELYN All right. If you say so. Oh dear. Right, I'll tell Amy. *(She descends the stairs)* Norris would be grateful if we could all assemble here in the sitting-room in five minutes. Thank you.

JOCELYN *goes out to the kitchen.*

BRINTON Why?

NORRIS *(belligerently)* Because. That's why.

BRINTON Fair enough.

NORRIS *goes off to the study.*

There is a slight pause. **WENDY** *re-packs her case a bit. She is a methodical packer.* **BRINTON** *watches her.*

BRINTON I...er... *(He coughs)*

WENDY Oh, hallo there.

BRINTON Look, I was listening to what you were saying yesterday about the house and what you were planning to do. With your dogs and so on. Well, I just wanted to say that I've lived here all my life. I was born here. And consequently I know this place better than anyone. And if... and if you should get the house, I want you to know that I'm very, very, very good with dogs. So if you do need a hand, don't forget me... Dogs love me, actually. They follow me everywhere. Extraordinary.

WENDY I won't be having the house.

BRINTON You won't?

WENDY I don't think it's been left to me after all. Anyway it's a little big.

BRINTON Well. Super. Look. Forget all that last bit, then. I loathe dogs. Can't stand them at all. Look, er... I just— *(He coughs)* I just happened to catch sight of you through the window as I was crouching in the nettles out there and I just had to draw you. Spur of the moment thing.

WENDY How lovely.

BRINTON Yes. Here. *(He removes his hand from his coat for the first time to reveal he is holding a sheet of sketching paper)*

BRINTON *hands the picture to* **WENDY**.

WENDY Oh. *(She studies the sketch)* Oh, yes. *(It is obvious from her expression that it is not a picture you can say an awful lot about)*

BRINTON Do you like it?

WENDY Yes. Yes. *(She pauses)* Yes. Is this how I look?

BRINTON To me. *(He coughs)*

WENDY Yes.

BRINTON It's caught you, I think.

WENDY It has. Yes. It has. May I keep it?

BRINTON Of course. Of course. It's for you. Dozens more where that came from.

WENDY I'll keep it very carefully. I promise.

BRINTON Don't tell everyone, will you? I don't want to make a habit of giving pictures away.

WENDY No.

BRINTON +++ Oh. *(At this point, for the first time, he catches sight of* **MORTIMER**'s *award on the piano)*

WENDY *watches* **BRINTON**. **BRINTON** *turns away sharply, aware of* **WENDY**'s *attention.*

WENDY Sorry?

BRINTON Nothing. I was just— +++

WENDY *opens her large case and places the picture carefully on top of her packing.*

(seemingly very pleased) It should travel OK.

AMY *enters from the kitchen, followed by* **JOCELYN**.

JOCELYN ...what do you mean, an accident? How could it have been an accident?

AMY It was.

JOCELYN What, all that milk and sugar and cornflakes? Don't be ridiculous.

WENDY Yes, it was really. It was an accident.

JOCELYN It was?

WENDY Yes.

JOCELYN Extraordinary. *(She looks suspicious)* I suppose we all ought to sit down. It's usual on these occasions, isn't it?

BRINTON What occasions?

JOCELYN Occasions like these.

They sit separately around the room. There is a silence.

BRINTON Why are we—?

JOCELYN Ssh. He won't be a minute. I expect.

After a second, **NORRIS** *enters. He has a grave manner befitting to the occasion. Underneath, though, there is an undoubted bubble of excitement. He looks at them grimly.*

NORRIS Now then. *(He walks in silence to one end of the room)*

BRINTON Where's he going?

JOCELYN Ssh.

NORRIS *turns dramatically.*

(softly) Don't be too long, will you, Norrie? Only Wendy's got a train to catch.

NORRIS Ladies and gentlemen, I am about to present to you a murderer. *(A slight dramatic pause)* As you're aware, over the past weekend, a whole chain of extraordinary, seemingly disconnected events has led inexorably to the fatal assault on the late Mortimer. Initially, as I say, a baffling series of events. At first sight, what was the possible connection between a wardrobe falling on a woman and an attack on a man at dead of night in his own study? Between a champagne glass filled with a potentially lethal mixture of disinfectant and an innocuous children's song? What could it be?

BRINTON I don't know, I give up.

NORRIS *(ignoring this)* Let us go back now, over the events as they occurred.

JOCELYN Not too far back, Norris.

NORRIS *(remorselessly)* Back to the start. Two weeks ago when Mortimer, angered by some irrational impulse, determined to leave this house and its contents to a near stranger. What consternation that caused. What a perfect motive for murder. Murder of the owner of the property? Possibly. Providing, that was, that the property had not already been left to the beneficiary. But what if it had? What if Mortimer had already drawn up the relevant documents, say, on musical manuscript paper, leaving everything to Wendy Windwood? Then it would be Wendy, rather than Mortimer, who became the focus of the murderer's intentions. Hence the events that followed her arrival. All of them events apparently, I say apparently, aimed against the woman who would finally inherit the house. Too late to do anything against Mortimer, for the die was cast. Who was it then, threatening the life of this innocent young woman? Was it Jocelyn? Desperate to preserve her home? Desperate that her family heritage should not pass into the hands of strangers purely on the whim of her half-crazed brother?

JOCELYN *shrugs, helpless to stop him.*

(wheeling on **AMY***)* Or was it Amy? Hoping one day to inherit for herself? She was, after all, the natural heir to the Chalke fortunes. Or was it Brinton?

BRINTON *(immediately)* No, it wasn't.

NORRIS Determined to preserve his own highly idiosyncratic way of life at any cost, even if the price was a brother's blood itself? Or was it me? Driven to desperate measures in an attempt to preserve my loved one's home?

JOCELYN *(softly)* Time's getting on, dear.

NORRIS Curious, then, that the murderer should suddenly switch their attack from Wendy to Mortimer. Perhaps they'd learnt subsequently that Mortimer had not made a will after all. In which case, it became imperative to stop Mortimer from making one. Or could there be another, far subtler explanation? What if the early attempts were not genuine attempts at all but fakes, designed to draw our attention away from the real crime. What then?

WENDY *and* **JOCELYN** *exchange a look.*

What if the brakes – you remember the brakes in the vehicle bringing her here – what if they had been tampered with during the journey and not before it? What if the wardrobe was designed not to kill but to distract? What if the switching of glasses was not accidental but deliberate? What if the victim was never Wendy but Mortimer all the time? Where then does suspicion fall? Perhaps on someone who was in the car with Mortimer and took the opportunity, whilst he'd stopped to deliver magazines to old Annie, to slip an adjustable spanner from her handbag and tamper with the brakes herself. Knowing, as she did, how little of the journey remained, and thus how mild the risk of danger to her own person would be. What if this same person, as soon as she was alone in her room, produced from that same handbag a small screwdriver? Who then, removing the retaining screws, allowed the wardrobe to fall on her? A fortunate escape indeed. And remember, as a pet shop owner, she had undoubtedly developed a natural manual dexterity. What if she deliberately poisoned her own glass and allowed, by simple sleight of hand, the switch to take place with Mortimer's glass? And what, finally, if, having been frustrated in this attempt, she was forced to take her final, drastic, brutal action? Clubbing down the man beside his own piano? Possibly hiding the murder weapon inside the instrument itself and, later, during the ensuing confusion, returning it to the study and tampering with the window in there. In which direction does all this evidence point? Why, to the only person in this room who stood to gain from Mortimer's death. The person whom, I contend, plotted that death from the very second she was informed of her legacy. That person, ladies and gentlemen, is Wendy Windwood.

A silence.

(facing **WENDY***)* What have you to say, then? Do you deny this? Can you deny it, Wendy Windwood?

WENDY *looks from one to the other of them in perplexity. Finally, she looks at* **JOCELYN** *who, unseen by* **NORRIS**, *gives* **WENDY** *an imploring look.*

WENDY *(with a sudden, despairing cry)* Yes. Yes, I did it. I did it.

NORRIS *looks triumphant.*

AMY She did it?

BRINTON Did she?

AMY She couldn't have done, she—

JOCELYN *(swiftly)* Norris, that was brilliant.

NORRIS Thank you.

JOCELYN Well done. Worthy of Martin Stonegate.

NORRIS Thank you.

WENDY *weeps.* **NORRIS** *moves to the front door.*

JOCELYN What are you doing?

NORRIS I'm going to summon the police.

JOCELYN Police?

BRINTON I don't think she did it at all.

JOCELYN *(fiercely)* Be quiet.

NORRIS Got to hand her over.

JOCELYN Norris, please, no.

NORRIS *opens the front door and steps outside.*

WENDY Now what are we going to do?

JOCELYN Shhh!

NORRIS *enters.*

NORRIS Where have they gone? There's nobody out here? There were dozens of them a minute ago.

AMY They went for lunch.

NORRIS *(incredulously)* Lunch? Lunch? This is a murder enquiry. I must warn you that anything you say during my lunch break will be taken down. Just a minute, they'll have left a man at the back. At the crime scene. By the broken window. I'll fetch him.

NORRIS *exits.*

WENDY What am I going to do? I can't be arrested for murder. Ollie would be furious. I didn't know he was going to call the police. What am I going to do?

JOCELYN *(a bit stumped)* Er—

A knock on the front door.

WENDY It's them. The policemen back from lunch.

JOCELYN Who is it, Brinton? Is it them?

BRINTON *(looking out of the window)* No, I think it's a taxi.

JOCELYN Thank God. He's early. *(To* **WENDY***)* Quickly. You must get to the station. Before he comes back. Wendy, I love you. You were wonderful, just wonderful. *(She hugs her)*

WENDY I did a little bit in *Hiawatha* last year.

AMY *(with some admiration)* Amazing.

BRINTON I don't get all this at all.

JOCELYN It's all right, Brinton, she didn't do it really.

BRINTON No, I didn't think she did.

JOCELYN Have you got everything?

WENDY Yes. Oh no, my other case.

At this point, the various alternatives come into play—

Either it's Brinton:

AMY I'll fetch it. It's in the kitchen.

JOCELYN No, I'll get it. Amy, you keep an eye out for Norris. Try and delay him.

AMY Right.

AMY *goes out to the study.* **JOCELYN** *goes off to the kitchen.*

BRINTON *(opening the front door; calling to the driver)* Hallo. She's just coming. *(To* **WENDY***)* Here, I'll take your case. *(He takes it)*

WENDY Excuse me, it was you that did it, wasn't it?

BRINTON Did what?

WENDY Killed Mr Chalke – Mortimer?

BRINTON Me?

WENDY You never did set off for that meeting, did you? At the Arts Society?

BRINTON Yes, I did.

WENDY On your bike?

BRINTON Yes.

WENDY In the dark?

BRINTON Yes.

WENDY Without your front light?

BRINTON Yes. *(He pauses)* How do you mean? *(He coughs)*

WENDY You didn't have your light because Amy borrowed it earlier. I saw it there on the table. It was a very dark night; you'd never have got to the village. You didn't go anywhere, did you? You just waited till everything was quiet and then sneaked back.

BRINTON *(defiantly)* How do you know?

WENDY I know you did. You're like Gilbert, I can tell when you're lying.

BRINTON What about the broken window, then? It could have been an intruder for all you know.

WENDY I don't think so. I don't think an intruder would bother breaking the window after he'd hit Mortimer on the head. Which he did do because I heard him. He'd have just legged it. Unless the intruder only wanted us to think he was an intruder.

There is a short pause while **BRINTON** *digests this.*

BRINTON Well, I didn't mean to.

WENDY And then there was that statue – Mortimer's award. I noticed you were surprised when you saw it on the piano there just now. That's what you hit him with, wasn't it? Then he grabbed it from you and you broke the window and ran. I put it back there. Last night before the police came. It's all right, I cleaned it first.

BRINTON I didn't, I never meant to… I just wanted some money to mend my roof. I didn't expect him to be there, creeping about in the dark. What on earth was he doing? Laughing at me like that? He should have been in here. Talking to you.

WENDY Don't worry. I won't tell anyone. *(She opens her bag)* Here.

BRINTON What's that?

WENDY *(producing the cycle lamp)* I'd put this back on your bike before you get nicked.

BRINTON Why? Why are you doing this?

WENDY Because… Because you…you once did something for me. Years ago.

BRINTON I did? What?

WENDY You can look out of windows as well, you know. *(She kisses him on the cheek)* Goodbye. And thank you.

BRINTON *is baffled. He coughs.*

JOCELYN *enters with the small case.*

JOCELYN Come on, come on. What are you playing at? Get in the taxi. *(She refers to the case)* This is still soaking wet. She didn't even dry it properly.

AMY *returns from the study hurriedly.*

AMY *(urgently)* He's coming back.

JOCELYN *(shooing the other two out of the front door)* Quickly.

BRINTON *and* **WENDY** *go out, followed by* **JOCELYN** *and then* **AMY**. *The front door slams.*

Or it's Amy:

AMY It's in the kitchen. Brin, can you get it?

BRINTON Me?

AMY Please. It's on the kitchen table.

JOCELYN Right. I'll try and delay Norris. Amy, you help Wendy with her case. Hurry up! Hurry up!

AMY Right.

JOCELYN *goes out to the study.* **BRINTON** *goes off to the kitchen.*

AMY *(opening the front door; calling to the driver)* She's just coming. *(To* **WENDY***)* Here, I'll take your case. *(She takes it)* I just wanted to say to you, I may get in touch.

WENDY Good. Excuse me, it was you that did it, wasn't it?

AMY Did what?

WENDY Killed Mr Chalke – Mortimer?

AMY What are you talking about? Look, I may ruin suitcases but I don't—

WENDY It was a silly little thing gave you away. While you were carrying on this morning, one of the things you did, you started humming a little song I wrote. "The Sausage Song". A stupid tune but quite catchy, isn't it?

AMY *is silent.*

Now, the only time I sang that in this house was last night. And the only way you could have heard it was if you were here. But you couldn't have been. You were at the cinema, weren't you? Apparently. So you couldn't have heard it.

AMY I could have heard it. From you. On another occasion.

WENDY No. I only sung it then.

AMY Well then. From Norris. He must have hummed it. He was here.

WENDY But he's tone deaf, isn't he?

AMY *doesn't reply.*

And then there was the statue – Mortimer's award. I noticed you were surprised when you saw it on the piano there just now. It's all right, I put it there. Last night, before the police came. I cleaned it first. That's what you hit him with, wasn't it? Then he grabbed it from you and you broke the window and ran. And you were never at the cinema, were you? Despite what your mother says.

There is a silence. **AMY** *thinks about it.*

Why? Why did you do it?

AMY Needed some money. That's all.

WENDY Just for you?

AMY 'Course.

WENDY No-one else?

AMY No.

WENDY Your mother?

AMY He was throwing us out. She needed... We had to live. She's old. He was there. In the dark. Waiting for me. Starting slapping me about. Bastard. Anyway. It could still have been an intruder.

WENDY I don't think so. I don't think an intruder would bother breaking the window after she'd hit Mortimer on the head. Which she did do because I heard her break it. She'd have just legged it. Unless the intruder only wanted us to think she was an intruder.

AMY Go and tell them, then. The police. If you're that certain.

WENDY I think sometimes we all deserve another start, don't we? It's only fair. *(She kisses her on the cheek)* Come and stay if you can, won't you? I think it would do you good. Really.

AMY *(noncommittally)* Yes.

BRINTON *returns holding* **WENDY***'s case gingerly.*

BRINTON Why is this all sticky? It's all sticky.

JOCELYN *returns from the study hurriedly.*

JOCELYN *(urgently)* He's coming back. Come on, come on. *(She shoos the others out of the front door)* What are you all playing at? Get in the taxi...

BRINTON *and* **WENDY** *go out, followed by* **JOCELYN** *and then* **AMY**. *The front door slams.*

Or it's Jocelyn:

JOCELYN Right. Amy, you go and fetch it. Brinton keep an eye out for Norris. Warn us if he's coming back.

BRINTON Me?

JOCELYN Quickly.

AMY *goes off to the kitchen.* **BRINTON** *goes off to the study.*

(opening the front door; to the driver) Hallo. She's just coming. *(To* **WENDY***)* Here, I'll take your case. *(She takes it)*

WENDY Excuse me, it was you that did it, wasn't it?

JOCELYN Did what?

WENDY Killed Mr Chalke – Mortimer?

JOCELYN What an extraordinary thing to say.

WENDY I know why you did it. You told me yourself this morning. For Norris, wasn't it? You'd do anything not to see him hurt.

JOCELYN How did you know?

WENDY No-one who's that fond of old detective films would ever get James Cagney muddled up with Edward G. Robinson. Not if she'd seen the film, that is.

JOCELYN Hell. I thought I'd been brilliant. I drove to the cinema especially, too. So I'd be seen and remembered. I even looked at the pictures outside to get some idea of the film.

WENDY It was the last night, though, didn't you say?

JOCELYN *(realizing)* Saturday night. They'd already changed the pictures.

WENDY And then there was the statue – Mortimer's award. I noticed you were surprised when you saw it on the piano there just now. That's what you hit him with, wasn't it? Then he grabbed it from you and you broke the window and ran.

JOCELYN I dropped Amy off – at the bus station café. And I thought, no, I can't just sit there calmly watching a movie with all this hanging over us.

WENDY Amy guessed it was you. She tried to cover up for you, didn't she? Saying she was at the cinema with you.

JOCELYN She shouldn't have done that. Anyway, I drove back. I was just getting out of the car. There was this flash of lightning and I saw Mortimer creeping about round the back of the house. He was carrying Amy's old giant doll. The one I made for her. I followed him. Then I realized what he was doing. To all of us. To Norrie. Playing games. Trying to make a fool of him. Laughing at us. I got so...so angry... I never dreamt I could get that angry. I just wanted to hurt him, like he was hurting us. Hurting Amy. *(She indicates the award)* How did it get there? Was it you put it there?

WENDY Last night. Before the police came. I cleaned it first, don't worry.

JOCELYN This is only your theory, you know. It could just as easily have been an intruder all the time.

WENDY I don't think so. I don't think an intruder would bother breaking the window after she'd hit Mortimer on the head. Which she did do because I heard her breaking it. She'd have just legged it. Unless the intruder only wanted us to think she was an intruder.

JOCELYN *(wryly)* If you're so sure, why haven't you told the police? Have me locked up?

WENDY Well, I know it's probably wrong of me but I think, quite honestly, that wouldn't help at all. There's far too many people who need you here. *(She kisses* **JOCELYN** *on the cheek)* Goodbye. And thank you.

AMY *returns with the small case.*

AMY *(referring to the case)* This is still a bit wet, I'm afraid.

BRINTON *returns from the study agitatedly.*

BRINTON *(urgently)* He's coming back.

JOCELYN *(shooing the other two out of the front door)* Quickly. Come on, get in the taxi.

JOCELYN *and* **WENDY** *go out, followed by* **AMY** *and then* **BRINTON.**

And then (whatever happens):

NORRIS *enters through the study door, slamming it behind him.*

NORRIS *(as he enters)* I've had it up to there with that lot, they've— *(He surveys the empty room)* What the—? *(He grasps the situation and runs to the front door which he flings open)*

JOCELYN *stands blocking his path.*

What's going on?

JOCELYN Norris, listen—

NORRIS What's going on?

There is the sound of the taxi driving away.

She's getting away! You're letting her get away!

JOCELYN Norris!

NORRIS *pushes* **JOCELYN** *aside and exits at a run.*

NORRIS *(as he goes; shouting)* Stop that car! Stop that car!

JOCELYN *comes back inside slowly.*

(offstage) What are you two playing at? You're aiding and abetting a murderer there! Stop that... My God!

NORRIS *comes back inside.*

(furiously, to **JOCELYN***)* Do you realize what you've done?

JOCELYN Norris.

NORRIS You've just made yourself an accessory after the fact.

JOCELYN Norris.

NORRIS The world's gone mad. First him out there...

JOCELYN Who?

NORRIS That constable. "Arrest her", I said, "she's confessed." "Hang on", he says, "I'm halfway through my sandwich." I mean, what's the matter with this country? No wonder we've slumped down the league table. Our whole moral code's shot to ribbons.

JOCELYN Norris...

NORRIS What?

JOCELYN Calm down. Just calm down or you'll have a stroke or something. A heart attack. Now sit down. Sit.

NORRIS *sits.*

That's better.

NORRIS My one chance, Joss. My one chance for glory and you've let her walk. I can't believe you'd do that.

JOCELYN Do you want to see her go to prison?

NORRIS Naturally.

JOCELYN Because she might have killed Mortimer?

NORRIS She did kill him. I proved she did. She confessed to it.

JOCELYN *(carefully)* Even supposing she did kill him, there are some might say she'd done us all a service.

NORRIS *(shocked)* Joss! This is your brother you're talking about!

JOCELYN Oh, come on. That from you of all people. He stopped being a brother a long time ago. He hated us all. He couldn't care less about us. He'd have seen us in the street without a qualm—

NORRIS Nonetheless—

JOCELYN ...and he loathed you most of all—

NORRIS ...the law must take its... *(Genuinely surprised)* Did he?

JOCELYN *(with difficulty)* Norrie. You mustn't pursue this any further. Really.

NORRIS Why not?

JOCELYN Because... Because she didn't kill him. Wendy. I'm sorry, but she didn't.

NORRIS How do you know?

JOCELYN *(awkwardly)* I just...sort of do. *(Feebly)* Intuition.

NORRIS What is this? Do you know something I don't? Are you covering up for someone?

JOCELYN No. Just...let it go. Please, Norrie.

NORRIS I'm sorry, Joss. I can't leave it like this. What are we going to do?

JOCELYN *(slightly irritably)* We're not going to do anything. We're just going to carry on with our lives. Mortimer's gone. Nothing else has changed. We'll eat, sleep, talk, play cards, endeavour to write, try to paint... What does it matter?

NORRIS It's all right for you lot. What about me?

JOCELYN Oh, I don't know, Norris. Go for a walk, read a book, learn to play the piano... I don't know. Get some art in your life. You'll feel so much better. Coffee?

NORRIS Tea.

JOCELYN Right.

JOCELYN *exits to the kitchen.*

NORRIS *is very depressed. He sits morosely. After a second he rises and wanders around aimlessly. He opens the piano lid and plays a note or two. He closes the lid again. He picks up* **JOCELYN**'s *book and flips the pages.*

NORRIS *(as he does this, disgustedly)* Read a book! Huh!

The piece of paper, **MORTIMER**'s *typewritten "list" falls out of the book.* **NORRIS** *picks up the list and prepares to replace it in the book, assuming it to be a book mark. Out of curiosity he glances at the paper.*

(eyes widening in excitement) My God! My God! *(His lips move as he reads the contents; then, softly)* Brakes, ladder, screws, bleach...

There is a loud knock on the front door. **NORRIS** *jumps. He hastily stuffs the sheet of paper into his pocket and replaces the book where he found it. Another knock.* **NORRIS** *goes to the front door. He peers out first and then opens the door.*

BRINTON *and* **AMY** *enter.*

BRINTON *(cheerfully)* Thank you.

NORRIS Come in. Come in.

AMY She's gone.

NORRIS Yes. *(He closes the door after them)*

JOCELYN *enters from the kitchen.*

JOCELYN Have you answered the—? Oh good. Do you want coffee, you two?

BRINTON Fine.

JOCELYN Amy?

AMY Yeah.

JOCELYN Please.

AMY Please.

JOCELYN *(detecting a change in* **NORRIS***'s manner since she last left the room)* You all right, Norris?

NORRIS Never felt better, thank you.

JOCELYN No?

NORRIS Never better. *(He stares at each of the others in turn, smiling knowingly)*

The others are each of them uneasy at **NORRIS***'s manner.*

I'll tell you something. Don't for a moment, any of you, consider this investigation is cut and dried. No matter what the police might say. Never for a minute. Enough said? *(He walks towards the study)*

JOCELYN Norrie, what are you talking about?

NORRIS Just call it fresh evidence. One of you knows what I'm talking about. One of you does.

NORRIS *exits.*

The others look at each other.

JOCELYN *(appalled)* Oh, dear.

They continue to stand staring at each other as...

...the curtain falls.

FURNITURE AND PROPERTY LIST

ACT I

Scene One

On stage: Fire irons
Table
Side table
Chairs
Grand piano. *On it:* sheets of music
Piano stool
Armchairs. *Under the cushion on one:* newspaper
Sofa
Sideboard. *In a drawer:* cards, labelled matchboxes full of matchsticks

Offstage: Umbrella (**Brinton**)
Norris's slippers (**Amy**)
Tray of tea things including cake (**Amy**)
Towel (**Jocelyn**)
Statuette (**Mortimer**)

Scene Two

Re-set: Tidy set a little

Set: Cocktail nibbles
Tray with six champagne glasses

Strike: Electric fire

Offstage: Small vanity case (**Wendy**)
Bicycle lamp (**Amy**)
Larger suitcase matching vanity case (**Amy**)
Champagne bottle (**Mortimer**)
Bicycle with bell (**Brinton**)

Personal: **Mortimer**: piece of paper
Norris: six screws
Norris: grubby handkerchief

ACT II

Scene One

Strike: Cocktail nibbles

Offstage: Doll's head (**Stage Management**)

Personal: **Mortimer**: piece of paper

Scene Two

Re-set: Clean **Mortimer**'s award and set on piano

If murderer is **Brinton**:

Re-set: **Brinton**'s bicycle lamp – in **Wendy**'s bag

Set: *On table*: five place settings for breakfast, two "finished with", one untouched, one with half-eaten piece of toast on plate, one with piece of toast for **Jocelyn**; packets of cereal, milk jug, sugar bowl, jar of marmalade; **Jocelyn**'s book with **Mortimer**'s piece of paper inserted

Strike: Doll's head

Offstage: Tray (**Amy**)
Wendy's cases. *In the large case*: cardigan. *In the vanity case:* tissue (**Wendy**)
Pot of tea (**Amy**)
Toast (**Amy**)

Personal: **Brinton**: sketch

LIGHTING PLOT

Practical fittings required: table lamps, electric fire with glow effect, "real fire" with glow effect
One interior. The same throughout

ACT I, Scene One

To open: Darkness

Cue 1 When ready (Page 2)
Bring up general interior lighting to suggest dark, cold, wet evening. Table lamps on. Electric fire with glow effect

Cue 2 **Jocelyn** starts to deal second card to each player (Page 26)
Blackout

ACT I, Scene Two

To open: General interior lighting. Table lamps on. "Real fire" with glow effect

Cue 3 **Mortimer** switches off overhead lights (Page 65)
Snap off overhead lights

Cue 4 **Wendy** sits; pause (Page 66)
Blackout

ACT II, Scene One

To open: Same setting as end of Act I

Cue 5 **Norris** looks out cautiously (Page 71)
Lightning

Cue 6 **Norris**: "It's pitch dark, I can't see—" (Page 72)
Lightning

Cue 7 **Wendy**: "Yes." (Page 73)
Overhead lights and lamps dim to glimmer

Cue 8 **Norris**: "...round this place in the dark." (Page 73)
Lightning

Cue 9 **Wendy**: "It could be any one of them." (Page 79)
Blackout

ACT II, Scene Two

To open: General interior lighting to suggest cold, sunny morning. Lamps and fire effect off

No cues

EFFECTS PLOT

Music cues are included for companies that (a) cannot have a real piano onstage or (b) do not have pianists amongst their acting strength and will require the actors to mime their piano-playing

ACT I

Cue 1 As curtain rises (Page 2)
Piano music (described on p. 1–3)

Cue 2 Door swings open (Page 3)
Wind and rain effects; music flutters on piano

Cue 3 **Norris** closes the door (Page 3)
Cut wind and rain effects

Cue 4 **Brinton** steps out of the front door (Page 4)
Wind and rain effects; music flutters on piano

Cue 5 **Mortimer** stabs at his music (Page 4)
Sound of sudden gust of wind; front door slams shut; cut wind and rain effects

Cue 6 **Norris**: "Anybody." (Page 10)
Telephone tings

Cue 7 **Amy** bangs the tea things down (Page 14)
Telephone tings

Cue 8 Scream from **Wendy** (Page 46)
Crash

Cue 9 **Amy** exits (Page 64)
Distant peal of thunder

Cue 10 **Wendy** plays the piano (Page 64)
Isolated notes on piano

Cue 11 **Norris**: "...we're ready." (Page 65)
Distant rumble of thunder

ACT II

Cue 12 As Scene One begins (Page 67)
Distant rumble of thunder

Cue 13 **Wendy** plays a chord, then plays and sings (Page 68)
Piano as pp. 68–70

Cue 14 **Wendy**: "Fizz, fizz, sizzle and fizz." (Page 69)
Enormous clap of thunder

Cue 15 **Wendy**: "...the pan are just—" (Page 69)
Loud clatter from kitchen

Cue 16 **Wendy**: "Right. Norris." (Page 71)
Thunder

Cue 17 **Wendy**: "Oh, dear." (Page 71)
Distant dinner gong

Cue 18 **Norris**: "It's pitch dark, I can't see—" Lightning (Page 72)
Thunder

Cue 19 **Norris**: "...round this place in the dark." Lighting (Page 73)
Thunder

Cue 20 **Wendy** plays the piano (Page 73)
Unsteady piano playing as pp. 73

Cue 21 **Wendy**: "Fizz, fizz, sizzle and—" (Page 73)
Loud crash from upstairs

Cue 22 **Wendy** plays the piano (Page 75)
Piano playing as pp. 75–76

Cue 23 **Wendy** stares at **Mortimer** in horror (Page 77)
Shattering glass like a window breaking

Cue 24 **Norris**: "...full blown murder now." (Page 78)
Low rumble of thunder

Cue 25 **Amy** plays the piano (Page 93)
Piano playing as p. 93

Cue 26 **Norris**: "What's going on?" (Page 114)
Sound of taxi driving away

Cue 27 **Norris** plays the piano (Page 116)
A note or two on the piano

Lightning Source UK Ltd.
Milton Keynes UK
UKHW02f2005100418
320830UK00007B/732/P